A TREASURY OF
MEDICAL HUMOR

- DOCTORS   • HOSPITALS   •DENTISTS
   • NURSES   • PATIENTS
   •EARLY AMERICAN MEDICAL HUMOR

Edited by

James E. Mye

THE LINCOLN-HERNDON PRESS, INC.

818 S. Dirksen Parkway

Springfield, Illinois 62703

A Treasury Of Medical Humor

Published by
      Lincoln-Herndon Press, Inc.
      818 S. Dirksen Parkway
      Springfield, Illinois 62703
      (217) 522-2732

Printed in the United States of America

LIBRARY OF CONGRESS CATALOGUING-IN-PUBLICATION DATA

      ISBN 0-942936-21-3
      Library of Congress Catalogue Card Number 92-071388
      Second Printing

Typography by
      Spiro Affordable Graphic Services
      Springfield, Illinois

TABLE OF CONTENTS

INTRODUCTION

The place, even necessity, for humor in nearly all phases of medical science is sometimes overlooked by professionals who frequently are so immersed in their profession that they find little or no time or place for laughter. But, as Norman Cousins said -- and every medical professional knows -- "Laughter not only provides internal exercise -- a form of jogging for the innards -- but it creates a mood in which other positive emotions can be put to work, too. In short, it makes it possible for good things to happen."

The strains, stresses, wear-and-tear of constantly dealing with malfunctioning human bodies takes enormous energy and often leaves the medical practitioner drained, not only of energy, but the pleasure and joy one expects from life. Hence, the following medically oriented and humorous stories, jokes, cartoons and essays are designed to give those in the medical profession a selection of the best humor that can produce hearty, life enhancing laughter, fun, joie de vivre.

It is well to recall the wise words of President John F. Kennedy: "There are three things that are real: God, human folly and laughter. The first two are beyond our comprehension, so we must do what we can with the third." Wise words indeed.

And if it seems difficult to laugh when you are constantly involved with that mysterious entity, the body (described by Samuel Butler as "A pair of pincers set over a bellows and a stew pan and the whole fixed on stilts") keep in mind that "He who laughs, lasts." And that, quite often, "Laughter is the best medicine" for those who are well as well as for those who are ill. "Laughter **is** the best medicine" may very well be the theme of this book, because laughter does us all, the sick and the well, great good.

So do use this book often -- for yourself, your staff and your patients, because it'll do you good. And do remember that postponing laughter just could bring on a severe case of hardening of the oughteries!

1

HUMOR ABOUT AND FOR DOCTORS

A serious disease, *obiose funest,* is carried by the Hindustani bagel fly, a recent entrant into this country. The fly poses special problems because it cannot be killed by swatting, by crushing or by chemical insecticides. The only known way to eliminate this deadly pest is to bore it to death while it watches the evening news report.

****

They say humor causes a tickle of the brain. . . and that laughter is the way to scratch it.

****

The doctor told her patient that laughter was free, legal, had no calories, no cholesterol, no preservatives, no carcinogens and was absolutely safe. And that she should go to the public library's humor section and select some pages of humor, five or six sample pages and take them at bedtime.

****

You know you are overweight and in need of serious dieting when the druggist looks at you and says, "No group discounts here, Sir."

****

Arkansas always takes its licks when it comes to malaprops. Here are a few medical bloopers from the mountains:
Many young girls enter the office complaining of "ministerial" trouble.
Pain in the lower quadrants offer, "I think I'm having overly trouble."
The hill woman told the doctor that she had once had an abdominal operation, "They took out all my female organdies."

Doctor's advice to elderly patients: "Lessen your tension and enjoy your pension."

****

NO, NO, I SAID SHOW ME YOUR OLD SPECTACLES

****

Dr. Robert Patton, the most prominent physician in town, was retiring and the newspaper planned an editorial tribute to him. A young reporter spent an entire day with him doing interviews. When the article appeared, however, Dr. Patton was shocked. There in black and white was the answer to the reporter's question about how he'd spent retirement: "I plan to work with established scholarship funds, give free advice to health clinics and other pubic activities."

****

At a recent medical convention, a speaker announced that the main occupational disease affecting Congressmen was, *"spendicitis."*

My doctor has recently been abducted into our Masonic order.

****

Terribly overweight, the man was told by his doctor to drastically reduce fatty foods, especially bread. The patient responded by shouting, "Cut out bread? How in hell am I gonna pick up the gravy?"

"You'll manage," responded the doctor. "Just keep in mind that dieting is the triumph of mind over platter. Just try to keep your will power dominant over your won't power."

****

"FOLLOW THIS DIET, MR. FIGBY, AND IN THREE MONTHS I WANT TO SEE TWO-THIRDS OF YOU BACK HERE FOR A CHECKUP."

****

Tracheotomy. The means of eliminating all oral conversation.

****

A Des Moines, Iowa physician has discovered a sure cure for nervousness in women. He tells them it's a sign of old age.

3

During World War II, a physician with the Marines diagnosed an illness of one of the men and wired the nearest hospital as to what he should do. He sent this message: "HAVE A CASE OF BERIBERI, ADVISE AS TO PROCEDURE."

A jokester at the hospital wired back: "GIVE IT TO THE MARINES, THOSE GUYS'LL DRINK ANYTHING."

****

A lady in San Francisco who had endured the tribulations of a gynecological "overhauling" set her reactions in rhyme:

They cut me up, and they cut me down,
And they take my insides out,
But there's some of me here,
And it's all the more dear
For that which I do without.
They wash my stomach out until
I wish it were not mine,
And all the while they sweetly smile
And say, "She's doing fine!"
They give me broth instead of food,
And junket for desserts,
They poke my tum and then, by gum,
The ask me if it hurts!
They tangle up my private works
With pains that will not pass,
And all the time, their faces shine...
You see, it's **only gas**!

(From *For Doctor's Only* by Francis Leo Golden. Frederick Fell, Inc., Publishers)

****

Her railroad ticket granted her a hangover in New York.

****

A South African doctor wrote about an epitaph he had seen in a local cemetery:

"In memory of my father: gone to join his appendix, his tonsils, his olfactory nerve, a kidney, an eardrum, and a leg prematurely removed by an intern who needed the experience."

****

Anesthesiologist: This is a physician who works in the operating room to delay your pain until such time as you get his bill.

4

A journalist asked a mother of several children how it felt to have a baby. She replied: "It's kinda like trying to pass a watermelon through a keyhole."

****

There had not been a physician in the town for a long time. Then, at last, a young man, fresh out of school, began to practice. His first job was to hammer his shingle beside the door to his office. An old man came by and stopped to watch him. Finished, the young doctor stepped down and reached for the old man's hand to introduce himself. Before he could speak the old guy said, "You seem like a right nice young feller, Doc, but I sure fear for you around here. Can't see how you'll ever make a livin' in this town ... . Why things is so danged healthy here that we couldn't begin our cemetery around here 'till the last doctor starved to death."

****

Doc, what should I do if my temperature goes up a point or more?
Sell!

****

Chico Marx, the member of the famed Marx Brothers, told the story about how a bout of stomach trouble had sent him to the doctor. The doctor prescribed plenty of milk and gave Chico a bottle of pills. "I'll stop by this evening to see how you're doing," the doctor said. "Meantime, drink at least four glasses of milk. Milk is the ticket to curing your trouble. So drink plenty of it."

That evening the doctor returned, examined Chico and said, "You're much better this evening. Just be sure you don't drink any milk. Not one glass. It's not for you."

"But, Doctor," Chico exclaimed, "only this morning you told me that milk was what I needed and that I should drink four glasses of it."

"Well, what do you know?" the doctor replied. "It certainly goes to show that we've made tremendous progress in medicine since the last time I saw you."

****

Malaprop No. 1: "They even had a throat spiritualist to examine me."

5

"Don't worry about those facial wrinkles," the doctor told his aging patient. "They're a good sign so long as they indicate where smiles have been."

****

An otolaryngologist had just returned from visiting his daughter who had married a dairy farmer. He called for his next patient who, if she'd been a cow, would have graded prime. He was so overcome by her hippopotamic proportions that he said, "Open your mouth, please, and say 'moo'."

****

Egomaniac. A physician who likes to talk about his problems while his brother physician stews and waits for a chance to talk about **his** problems.

****

"I once had a patient with marvelous eyesight," the optometrist told his nurse. "That man could see snow before anyone else was aware of it."
"Really," his nurse replied, "How do you account for that, Doctor?"
"Well," the optometrist replied, "the only thing I could figure was that he had excellent ice sight."

****

Medical terminology for sunburn: A fry in the ointment.

****

You know you've made the right decision to take up jogging when on your first try at it, you have more jiggle than jog.

****

"Please, Doc, like I said, my hair keeps fallin' out, what can you give me to keep it in?"
"A shoebox."

****

It has been said that we live on one-third of what we eat and the fat farms live on the rest.

****

The young man entered the Ice Cream Palace and asked, "What kinds of ice cream do you have?"

"Vanilla, chocolate, strawberry," the girl wheezed as she spoke, patted her chest and seemed unable to continue.

"You got laryngitis?" the young man asked sympathetically.

"Nope," she whispered, "just vanilla, chocolate and strawberry."

****

Penis: A well-centered male sexual organ that serves as the main subject of conversation of some males, especially in universities.

****

Mark Twain was asked if there was anything in all this world worse than having a toothache and an earache at the same time. "Yep," replied Twain, "There is. Having rheumatism and St. Vitus Dance."

7

DEATH: What, in the end, the patient does, some say to humiliate the physician. Physicians dislike and rarely use this word, just as they shun songs with titles like, *"Nearer My God To Thee."*

****

What did the skeleton say to his buddy, both in the medical hospital display case? "Y'know, if we had any guts we'd rattle our bony asses out of here."

****

One thing sure...you can overdo this dieting business. Just see what happened to a gal named Lena.

> That skinny gal named Lena
> Bought herself a vacuum cleaner.
> But she got in the way
> Of its suction one day
> Since then, nobody has seen her.

****

Vagina: The font of it all.

****

A man went to a California fat farm, mainly for rest and recreation. Once there, he discovered that he was expected to exercise.

He refused, saying, "I came here to read and rest and I ain't agonna exercise at all."

Well, he spent a pleasant, do-nothing week and then checked out. At the front desk, just after paying his bill, the manager begged him to exercise just a bit. "Just bend down, keep your knees stiff and touch your valise...I need you to do that to keep my reputation, my record clear." The man bent over and said, "Now, I'm touching it, just to oblige you. What now?" "Open it," said the manager, "and give me back my towels."

****

Writing on the cast of a broken arm or leg has become a national pastime. Here are a few dillies:

> So-o, plastered again, eh?
> You put on a rotten show but the cast was first rate.
> Nothing more than a plaster of Paris-ite.
> This is the only time I saw (plaster of) Paris.

8

"I THINK I FOUND WHAT'S CAUSING THAT IRRITATION ACROSS YOUR SHOULDER BLADES, MR. HARRISON."

****

Quack: A physician who disagrees with our diagnosis.

****

Did you hear about the man who swallowed a mouse while dozing on the couch? Well, he did and his wife rushed to the phone and called their doctor. "Doctor, please come quickly. My husband just swallowed a mouse and he's gagging something fierce."

"I'll be there right away," the doctor said. "Meantime, keep waving a piece of cheese over his mouth to attract the mouse up and out of there."

When the doctor arrived, he entered to see the wife waving a piece of smoked herring over her husband's mouth.

"Madam, I told you cheese, not herring, to lure the mouse."

"I know it, Doc," she replied, "but first I got to get the danged cat out of him."

Bob Hope never has to diet. He just stays thin. Perhaps the reason lies with the bands he travels with. On his last gig, they were having dinner and when he lowered his head to say grace and then looked up, the waiter was serving dessert!

****

I loved my wife
I hated to leave her,
But what can you do
With typhoid fever.

****

Terribly overweight, the man went to a spa known for its rigid promise of phenomenal weight reduction. At his first meal, the waitress served him a sandwich with the thinnest sliced bread he'd ever seen. Between the slices of bread was a morsel of ham. He called the waiter over. "Did you slice this ham?" he asked.
"No, Sir. The chef did that."
"Well, he darned near missed it."

****

An attractive young girl accepted an invitation to visit a U.S. Navy ship. In the company of a handsome young medical officer, she asked if he had a specialty.
"I'm a naval surgeon, Ma'am," he said.
"Really? A naval surgeon? My goodness, what'll you boys think of next."

****

"My hair keeps falling out, Doc, what can I do?"
"Step to one side!"

****

The doctor was treating a patient who was always keyed-up, deadly serious and rarely at ease. She advised the patient to take life less seriously because neither he nor anyone else would ever get out of it alive.

****

Parachuting -- jumping to contusions.

Malaprops, malaprops. Medicine is full of them. Here are a few from a physician in Virginia.

"I couldn't pass my water so the doctor installed a casket in me."
"My headaches lead me to believe I got science trouble."
"They called in a lung spiritualist to examine me."
"Then they dragged out a horoscope machine and looked at my stomach."
"I got bit by a mad dog and they gave me rabbi shots."
"The doc told my wife that the pains in her belly were caused by her ovals."

****

"Doctor Penning, I've been unable to get pregnant. Would you advise me to try artificial insemination?"
"Absolutely not. I've seen lots of babies born that way and haven't liked what I saw. I figure it's just another case of 'spare the rod and spoil the child.'"

****

"Doctor, I feel I am coming down with something!"

(More Over Sexteen, J.M. Elgart, 1953)

Dr. Shriver advised his patient, overwhelmed with worries, to do all his worrying during a specific half hour of the day...and then to take a nap at that time.

****

"Doctor, my brother Eddie is in the hospital. You're his physician, so can you tell me what his problem is?"
"His is a case of Bleedin' Seenims."
"My goodness, that sounds terrible. What is it?"
"It **is** terrible. Your brother was in bed with another man's wife and the husband came in, seenim' and bleedin' followed!"

****

Dr. Peter Bryan was a great braggert. A fellow surgeon described his conceit with these words, "If bullshit was music, he'd have a brass band!"

****

Doctor's advice to a young patient: "Vice is nice but a bit of virtue...won't hurtchue."

****

STEADY DOES IT

The doctor's working on a case,
          One must admire his poise.
He works with dedicated zeal,
          It's work that he enjoys.

The doctor's working on a case,
          As anyone may see.
He has a certain touch, a flair,
          And great capacity.

He's systematic, thorough, sure,
          Experienced and deft.
The doctor's working on a case --
          There's just one bottle left.

****

"Quit worrying," Dr. Peters told his patient. "Why pay interest on trouble before it is due?"

12

THE DOCTORS

Nowadays there's little meaning
For a person to be gleaning
When a man attaches "Doctor" to his name --
He may be a chiropractor
Or a painless tooth extractor --
He's entitled to the title just the same.

Or perhaps he is a preacher
Or a lecturer or teacher,
Or an expert who cures chickens of the pip;
He may keep a home for rummies,
Or massage fat people's tummies,
Or specialize in ailments of the hip.

Everybody is a "doctor,"
From the backwoods herb-concocter
To the man who takes bunions from your toes;
From the frowning dietician
To the snappy electrician
Who shocks you loose from all the body's woes.

So there's very little meaning
For a sufferer to be gleaning
When a man attaches "Doctor" to his name.
He may pound you, he may starve you,
He may cut your hair or carve you,
You have got to call him Doctor all the same!
(From *What the Queen Said*, Stoddard King. Doubleday Doran
& Co., Garden City, NY, 1931)

****

Seymour Persky, Chicago, IL, asks, "What do you call a geriatric
gynecologist?" Answer: A spreader of old wives' tales.

****

A career in proctology is that rare profession in which the M.D.
starts at the bottom and stays there!

****

Doctor: You're in good health, Mr. Johnson, You'll live to be
           80.
Patient: Doc, I am 80.
Doctor: See, what did I tell you.

"How do you do? I'm the house 'proctologist' --"

****

NOUNS OF ASSEMBLAGE

From Sarasota, Fl, Jack Mueller offers these collective nouns:

A rash of dermatologists.

A clot of hematologists.

A murmur of cardiologists.

A stream of urologists.

A pile of proctologists.

A poke of gynecologists.

An acher of bacteriologists.

A vessel of vascular surgeons.

New England doctors are known for their thrift. Here's what we mean, from **What the Old Timer Said.** Allen R. Foly. Stephen Green Press, Battleboro, VT.

This concerns a shrewd but kindly Vermont doctor who had spent all his practice in a small community and, because of his age, was about to take in sail. He was looking for some young doctor to buy him out and consulted the Dean of the Medical School at the University of Vermont. He told his story, warning the Dean that he wanted his people to have a good doctor, and the Dean said he had just the right young man in mind. He sent the young doctor to look over the proposition and the young man found a very comfortable house, including an office and a little lab, a barn and garden and fruit trees, and apparently a very good practice which the old doctor offered to sell, "lock, stock and barrel," at a very attractive price, allowing he knew something about the difficulties of getting started in a practice.

The young doctor was a bit skeptical. Observing what seemed to be a very comfortable living he wondered how this had been accomplished in a small community with a scattered population and no great signs of wealth. He asked the old doctor if his practice had always been on the up-and-up, or if he'd had to eke

out by doing anything not quite -- well, not quite . . .

"I'm glad you asked, son," the old doctor said, "and I'll be honest with you. I've never done anything irregular in my practice. It's all a question of thrift and attention to detail.

"I'll give you an illustration. In the summertime the folks around here think they ought to take a vacation, and they'll pack up and go off to the city or the beach and come back a week or two later all tired out and a lot poorer than when they left. My wife and I have never done that. Once in a while we may go to the state medical meeting, but the rest of the time we stay right here. Two or three times during the summer, on some of those lovely days that God gives us here, we close up the house and office, pack a picnic lunch, and go off for the day and gather herbs.

"Come fall, when my wife has to have a fire in the kitchen stove anyway, so it doesn't cost any extra, we put those herbs in a big kettle on the back of the stove and brew up a good old-fashioned spring tonic. We've always been saving of our bottles and we get them out, wash them and sterilize them, and bottle up that tonic. Then we make up some labels, stick them on the bottles, and put the whole lot away in the closet. And it hasn't cost us a cent!

"Then in the spring of the year I'll meet one of my patients and I'll say, 'Sue, you don't look too well. What's the matter?'

"'Doctor,' she'll complain, 'I'm all run down. Never felt so played-out. Got my spring cleaning started but don't know as I'll ever finish it.'

"'Sue,' I'll say, 'I think what you need is some old-fashioned spring tonic. On the way home why don't you go by the house and tell my wife you want a bottle of our tonic.'

"Now that's only a dollar and a quarter, son, but it's a dollar and a quarter and it's clear profit. A month or so later, I'll run into Mrs. ___ again and I'll say, 'Why, Sue -- how much better you look! That tonic was just what you needed.'

"'Yes, Doctor,'" she'll say, 'never felt better in my life.'

"'Now, Sue,' I'll say, 'this is just the time in life when you ought to come around for a physical check-up. Don't wait 'til you've got one foot in the grave and expect the doctor to pull you through. 'Bout your time in life we expect the changes, Sue, and we'll make an appointment right now. And by the way, when you come be sure to bring a specimen.'

"And that's the way, son, we've always got our bottles back."

A psychiatrist reported that a patient of his, an old man, worried so much about his debts that the hair began to fall out of his wig.

****

There's a doctor in Cincinnati who is so conceited about his personal charm that when he takes a women's pulse, he subtracts ten beats for his personality.

****

The doctor entered the patient's room with a grim look on his face. "I've good news for you, Mr. Jacobs, ... and bad news."
"What's the bad news?" the patient asked in a choked voice.
"We have to remove both legs."
"And the good news?"
"The patient in 634 wants to buy your slippers."

****

Doctor Edwards talks too darn much! And he talks too fast, listens too slow and always winds up with at least one foot in his mouth.

****

A woman came into the doctor's office and complained of a problem. "I'm pretty active socially, doctor, and my problem causes me real embarrassment. You see, I have an inordinate amount of pain in my stomach and pass a lot of gas. True, it has no odor and I control it so it makes no noise, but I know it is there and it makes me uncomfortable in the presence of others. Can you help me?"
The doctor nodded his head, gave her some pills and told her to come back in thirty days.
Well in two weeks the old girl was back, madder than a wet hen! "Doctor, what on earth was in those pills?" she screamed. "Now I smell terrible! What about that?"
The doctor looked at her, smiled, then said, "Good. Now that your nose is working fine, we have to get your hearing back to normal."

****

A beginner psychiatrist advertised as follows: "Satisfaction guaranteed or your mania back."

"YOUR NEW DIET WILL BE SIMPLE. IF IT TASTES GOOD, SPIT IT OUT."

****

Doctor: "Nurse, I've concluded that woman is nothing but a rag, a bone and a hank of hair."

Nurse: "You may be right, Doctor. But I've arrived at the opinion that man is nothing but a brag, a groan, and a tank of air."

****

Four physicians were enjoying coffee in the hospital coffee shop. They were discussing their humble, impoverished boyhoods with their poor families.

"Why," one doctor said, "we were so poor the garbage man would come by and ask, 'Pick-up or delivery?'"

"You think you were bad off? Let me tell you something! We were so blamed poor that my sister got married just so we'd have some rice in the house."

"Man, you were rich!" the third doctor remarked. "In our house, burglars would actually break into the house and leave things."

"You guys were on Easy Street," the third doctor remarked. "One time our banker came by and demanded his calendar back!"

18

"Doc, there's a feller outside with a wooden leg named Brown."
"What's he call his other leg?"

****

"Doctor, I'm so worried about those hormone pills you gave me," the woman said to her physician. "I just don't know what to do."
"Now calm down, Ma'am, and tell me the trouble."
"Well, those hormones have caused hair to grow on my chest!"
"Really? But tell me, Ma'am, how far down does the new hair extend?"
"To my testicles!"

****

Two country doctors who practiced in the hills of Arkansas were discussing the explosion of births, now world-wide. One physician said, "Why, Jonas, Thiseyer birth thang is agettin' so bad that perty soon they ain't goin' to be room for ever'body! There'll be standin' room only!"
"Well, Jacob," Doc Jonas replied, "that sure oughta slow 'em down some!"

****

Dr. Stewart Frank was an excellent organ player who was scheduled to give a jazz concert that was advertised as follows: "Come and see Dr. Stewart Frank and his swinging organ."

****

Psychiatrist: Mind-sweeper.

****

PROGRESS

A nutty old doc name of Green,
Thought he'd try out a brand new vaccine,
Gave himself an injection
That destroyed the infection,
It even grew hair on his bean.

****

Doc drinks to your health when he's with you.
He drinks to your health when alone,
He drinks to your health so terribly much,
That he's actually ruining his own!

Dr. Edgar tells his patients not to worry. "Worry," he says, "will get you to only one place ahead of time...the cemetery."

****

DR. KEY AND MRS. HARRIS

I've always liked the story they tell about old Dr. Key who lived in Greenville.

There was a rather scatter-brained lady in Greenville whom we'll call Mrs. Harris. She was probably the world's worst driver. Had one accident after another. One day she came out of a side street and ran slam-bang into Doc's car, denting the front fender badly.

"Oh, Dr. Key!" she exclaimed. "I'm awfully sorry."

"That's perfectly all right, Mrs. Harris," he said in his slow, drawling voice. "It was all my fault."

"Why, Dr. Key! I don't know why you say that. I'm sure it was entirely my fault."

"No, Mrs. Harris; it was my fault. I'll take the entire blame."

"But why is it your fault? I ran into you, didn't I?"

"Yes, you did. But I saw you driving down town half an hour ago, and I had plenty of time to take my car home and put it in the garage, but like a damn fool, I didn't do it!"

(Excerpt from *Just For the Fun of It*, 1954, written by Carl Goerch, used with permission of the Estate of Carl Goerch).

****

You think Doctor Jasper is smart? Well, I sure don't. I figure he's about as sharp as a rubber tack.

****

The nurse came rushing into Dr. Peters' office shouting, "Dr. Peters, something terrible has happened. You just finished examining Albert Thomas and gave him a clean bill of health. He dropped dead right outside the office door."

"Quick," yelled Dr. Peters, "turn him around so's it looks like he was just entering the office."

****

"Too many of us worry about the future," Dr. Smith explained, "Why open your umbrella before it starts raining?"

****

Psychiatrists don't have to worry so long as other folks do.

Sam Smith was shaving one morning when the can of shaving cream slipped for his hand and struck the toilet seat, scratching it. Knowing how particular, Mary, his wife of 40 years, was about the bathroom, the old boy quietly slipped downstairs, found some paint that was just the right color and quickly repainted the seat.

Late for work, he then hurried out, forgetting to leave a note about the seat. Thus, when Mary awoke and went to the bathroom, she found herself stuck to the seat.

Unable to move, she sat there crying until her husband came home for lunch. Apologizing profusely, Sam unscrewed the seat and helped poor old Mary into bed, face-down, of course.

"What are we going to do?" Mary wailed. "I can't spend the rest of my life wearing a toilet seat!"

"Don't worry," Sam assured, her, "I'll call the doctor. He'll know what to do."

Sam called the family physician but didn't tell him what had happened. He explained that there was no way his wife could go to the doctor's office. Reluctantly, the doctor agreed to stop by on his way home.

Sam let the doctor survey the situation from the door. Poor Mary had hoisted herself on hand and knees so the physician could see her huge. . .dilemma.

Sam asked, "Well, doc, you see why I called? What's your judgment?"

Stroking his chin, the doctor said, "I think it's a beauty...but why did you buy such a cheap frame to put it in!"

****

Here is the kind of remedy for the common cold that will appeal to most sufferers. It was suggested by Dr. Richard Gordon and appeared in the *Atlantic Monthly.*

At the first sign of a cold, go to bed with a bottle of whiskey and a hat. Place the hat on left-hand bedpost. Take a drink of whiskey and move hat to right-hand post. Take another drink and shift hat back again. Continue until you drink the whiskey but fail to move the hat. By then the cold is probably cured.

****

Finished with his examination and given a good report, old Stan Kenyon said to the physician, "Thanks a million, Doc. I'm sure glad to know I'm OK. And you know what? Tonight I'm going out on the town and paint it red."

"Well, you want to think that over," the doctor replied. "I doubt that you've got the brush for it."

21

"CHEER UP, REVEREND. WE'LL HAVE YOU UP AND BACK ON YOUR
KNEES AGAIN IN NO TIME."

****

An old farmer married a young girl but was unable to keep up with her. So he sought advice from his doctor.

"The next time you are out in the field," the doctor advised, "plowing or disking or harvesting or whatnot, and you feel the need for sex with your wife, just quit what you're doing and go to the house."

"I tried that, Doc. Doesn't work because by the time I walk to the farmhouse, I forgot what I came for...and when I remember, I'm just too derned tired for it."

"Well, why don't you take your shotgun to the field with you and, when you want your wife, fire the gun and let her come to you on that signal?"

Some weeks later the two met on the street. "So how did things work for you with your wife?" the doctor asked.

"First rate...the first week. Then hunting season started, and she hasn't got back home yet."

****

A witty physician once told a patient, suffering from arthritis, that he was "suffering from twinges in the hinges."

"Please, tell me, Doc...am I gettin' better?"
"How should I know? I think so...but to be sure...let me feel your purse."

"Doc, I'm sure there's somethin' wrong with my stomach."
"Not to worry. Keep your coat buttoned and nobody'll notice it."

"Doc, I got to tell you...every derned bone in my body aches. What should I do?"
"Pray! And be glad you're not a herring!"

****

Wisdom: Practicing psychiatry without faith in God is something like meeting a hungry beggar and giving him a toothpick.

****

Old Joe Flannigan, well past sixty years, married a very young girl and then left for their honeymoon. When they returned home, the young bride rushed off to her husband's doctor.
"Doctor," she shouted at him, "Just what kind of operation did you perform on my husband before we were married? I have to understand just what it was you did to him!"
"Oh, it was a common enough operation for men of his age. We fixed him up with a set of monkey glands."
"I should have guessed that," the young bride said, "Because during our entire honeymoon all he did was sit around, eat peanuts and scratch his back."

****

Joe Cantrall was close to eighty years old and thought it was time to have his annual visit to his doctor. In the office, the doctor said, "Well, Mr. Cantrall, I see you're still kickin'."
"Yep! Still kickin' but I ain't raisin' much dust. And what I raise ain't risin' very high."

****

Psychiatrists say one should not keep too much to himself. Strange as it may seem, the IRS agrees.

****

Psychiatrists have said that girls often marry men who are like their fathers. No doubt that is why mothers weep at their weddings.

23

The nurse brought a pair of pajamas to Joe Tompkins in Room 816. Unfortunately the pants were fit for a boy not a man but Joe didn't know how to go about telling the nurse of her mistake. So when she came in and asked if he was comfortable, he replied, "These here trousers remind me of the ball room at the Boardman Funeral Home."

"But, Mr. Tompkins, there is no ball room at Boardman's Funeral Home."

"That's what's wrong with these pants."

****

"How old are you, Mr. Hathaway?" the nurse asked him while filling out his Medicare form.

"I'm so danged old I can remember back when people stopped spending when they ran out of money!"

****

The physician prescribed suppositories for his elderly patient and suggested that he return one week later. The patient came back on time and the doctor asked, "Did you take the suppositories as I told you to do?"

"I certainly did, Doctor, and I can tell you this...they tasted terrible!"

"What? Tasted? You mean you swallowed them?"

"Sure! What'd ya think I did with them? Shove 'em up my ass?"

****

Unfair it may be...but a cynic once said that a psychiatrist is nothing more than a talent scout for a mental institution.

****

The doctor had finished examining his patient and began to talk to him. "Mr. Paul, I find very little wrong with you. You are in surprising good health despite your terribly overweight condition. My advice to you is to give up those intimate little dinners for two until you can find another person to eat with."

****

Back when doctors did not have an answering service but took all calls, at home or office, Doctor James Pegasus was awakened at 3 A.M., by a patient. "I can't sleep, Doc. Something is wrong and I just...can't...sleep. Can you help me!"

Dr. Pegasus replied in a sleepy, fuzzy voice, "Hold the phone and I'll sing you a lullaby."

It's true that psychiatrists add to your mental balance...but they sure reduce your bank balance.

****

Old Doctor Phineus Jones, notoriously absent-minded, stopped at the usual neighborhood tavern, walked to the bar and ordered his usual drink. Seated next to him was an awfully friendly gal who invited him to buy her a drink. He did. "You married?" she asked.

"Nope," Doc Jones replied.

"Live near here?"

"Yep."

"Would you like me to come home with you?"

"How much?"

"Fifty bucks an hour. Ninety bucks for an hour and a half. Two hundred for all night."

"OK," said the doctor. "Let's go."

When they entered his apartment, the gal turned to Doc Jones and asked, "Now what would you like me to do first?"

He looked at her, then looked around the room and said, "Please start with the windows."

****

Dr. Jim Graham had just ended an inconclusive and ferocious argument with a fellow gynecologist. Here is how he handled it. "George, I got one last suggestion to make. Why don't you just go on around the block twice and come back once!"

****

Dr. Hugh Nesbitt was long retired and more than a bit bored. Just for old-times' sake and overcome with nostalgia, he decided to visit the old brothel he had known as a young physician many years ago. So he drove past it and, miracle of miracles, the place looked the same. That night, he went back. Inside the place looked the same, too, but the girls and the madam had changed. "Madam," he began, "I'd like the most expensive girl in the house, if you please."

"I sure enough do please," the madam said, grinning. "But, Pop, you must be ninety years old! Right?"

"Pretty close. I'm ninety-one."

"Well, old man, forget it! You've had it!"

"I have? What a lousy memory I've got! So tell me. How much do I owe you?"

Podiatrists tell us that women's feet are getting larger and larger. Could it be that the growth comes from trying to fill men's shoes?

****

I feel sorry for my patient in 318...the poor thing is so skinny she could lie under a clothesline and not get sunburned.

****

Dr. Ernest McTigue, a specialist in obstetrics, appeared before the state medical convention shortly after arriving in town on a very small plan, a substitute for the large passenger plane normally used. He opened his lecture in this way:

"I arrived in town on a small plane, so small my ten-year-old boy would have rejected it as a plaything. It was something! It had a luggage rack on the roof and a bug screen on the windshield. The pilot wore scarf and goggles. There was no food service but they posted a request that each passenger bring a covered dish. Believe it or not, there was a notice above the oxygen mask stating that it was coin operated. And that pilot made four stops along the way, two of them were for directions! I tell you...it was so-o-ome trip."

****

A tried-and-true medical aphorism has it that nothing is more conducive to payment of an overdue doctor's bill than a new ailment.

****

Mrs. Edgar Thomas was a good and life-long friend of Doctor Werner Baugher, who did oil paintings of all kinds for a hobby. One day Mrs. Thomas suggested that her friend, Dr. Baugher, paint her portrait. This seemed such a good idea to the doctor that he agreed.

The first session, Mrs. Thomas asked the doctor to paint her in the nude. And, since they were old friends in every way, Dr. Baugher agreed. "However," he told her, "I got to keep my socks on because I'll need a place to keep my brushes."

****

The most extreme case of specialization we've heard of is the Washington, D.C. situation where one doctor only treats U.S. Senators. He refuses to make "House" calls.

Doc Halliday was asked what he thought of the latest women's fashion, short skirts and low-cut blouses. "I really don't think I'm qualified to answer that," he said.

"But you are! You're a doctor and know about such things."

"Not in this case," said Doc Halliday. "Insufficient evidence!"

****

The medical journals didn't report it, but the story goes that a man paid no attention to an inordinately long hair that grew out from his nostril. He developed hay fever one year and flogged himself to death sneezing!

****

A famous Chicago physician had an enormous art collection of inestimable value that he kept displayed in his apartment. Although elderly, he was quite a womanizer, and very successful at it, too. He would ask a lovely lass out to dinner, then to his apartment to view his collection. Invariably they would ask, "Doctor, what do you plan to do with this marvelous collection?" He would reply, "My will states that the entire collection goes to whomever is with me at the time of my death."

And do you know...that old boy has had some truly wonderful nights!

****

Nature seems to know what she is doing but...there are times when it does seem that she created mankind for the benefit of the medical profession.

****

"I barely pulled him through," Doctor Edmonds told his associate. "He was as close to death as the hair on the skin of a chicken's tooth."

****

The country doctor advised his teen-age son about girls: "Son, kissin' wears out. Cookin' don't."

****

Have you ever wondered why psychiatrists are called "shrinks?" Could it be because of what they do to our wallets?

"IT NEEDS A REST."

****

A doctor in Cedar Rapids was examining an effusive old dame who seemed filled to the brim and beyond with words. He was forced to sit and listen to lengthy descriptions of ill after ill after ill. At last he quieted her, made out a prescription and led her to the door.

"But, Doctor, you couldn't have finished with me. Why, you haven't even looked at my tongue to see if it was coated."

"My dear Mrs. Windpack...one never looks for grass on a racetrack."

****

Psychiatrists see some mighty strange people. Consider the man who entered the psychiatrist's office, removed a bag from his pocket, extracted tobacco from it and stuffed that tobacco into his right ear.

The psychiatrist watched with great interest, finally remarking, "Mighty wise of you to come to see me, Mr. Tompkins. You belong here. And just how can I help you?"

"Got a light, Doc?"

The job of a psychiatrist is to discover what makes you tick before you blow up.

****

A perennial bum had just about worn out his only pair of britches. Winter was approaching and he needed to beg a new pair. So he noticed a doctor's sign on a house, and walked to the door, knocked and a woman opened it. "Doctor in, Ma'am?" the bum asked.

"Yes," the woman says.

"Would you please ask him if he's got an old pair of pants he could give me? I'm about to fall out of these."

"Sorry, I couldn't do that," the woman replied.

"But why not? I don't care if they're old."

"The problem is, I'm the doctor."

****

"Put your brains in gear before you put your mouths in motion," the psychiatrist advised the unhappily married couple.

****

A drummer on tour broke down with a horrendous problem that needed immediate surgery. The physician operated on him and saved his life, later presenting him with a bill for fifteen hundred dollars.

The drummer was shaken. "Doctor, I can't afford that kind of bill. I'm just a simple musician." So the doctor says, "I understand. Just give me a thousand and we'll call it square."

"Still too much for me, Doc. Much too much." So they bicker and bargain and the doctor says, "Well, I'm tired of hassling this way. So forget the bill. I'll donate the cost of it all."

"Mighty nice of you, Doc." And the doctor says, "But if you knew you couldn't pay my fee, why come to me. You could have gotten a less expensive doctor."

"I know, I know, Doctor," the musician replied, "but where my health is at stake, money is no object."

****

They say Richard the Lion-Hearted was the first survivor of a transplant.

****

People often go to a psychiatrist slightly cracked but not busted.

29

Representative Joe Kolgore of Texas tells of a banker who went to his doctor to get a physical examination. After extended tests, the doctor said, "Sir, this much I can tell you...you're sound as a dollar."

"Oh my gawd," screamed the banker, "is it bad as that?" And he passed out.

****

Old Doctor Mathers, in rural Mason County, Illinois, said, "Since I don't know what women's styles are going to be like twenty years from now, it's darned hard to decide just where a baby girl should be vaccinated."

And old Doctor Mathers used to tell each new mother not to worry about the baby...that she should just remember to keep one end full and the other end dry....

****

It's for certain that you can carry this politeness thing too far. Just take a look at this obstetrical case.

This is the story of a pregnant woman, who complained to her doctor that she was afraid her unborn child might grow up to be rough and coarse like her husband, and what could she do to prevent that.

The doctor advised that every morning when she got up, she should tap her finger on her belly and repeat the words, "BE POLITE, BE POLITE, BE POLITE," and the same thing before going to bed at night. This, he assured her would have the correct impression on the unborn child to be polite.

She carried out the doctor's orders to a 'T.' After the eighth month she was anticipating the birth of the child. It was nine months, and still the child wasn't born. Ten and eleven months passed, and finally a year, and still she hadn't given birth.

In alarm, she returned to the doctor. He examined her and then put her under the fluoroscope to see what was wrong inside, and there he beheld the strangest sight ever known to medical science. There he saw two babies, twins, each one pointing to the opening and saying to the other, "After you," and the other would reply, "No, after you...."

****

Definition of rheumatism: Nature's first weather bureau.

A saleslady stopped by the doctor's office on the way home. "Doctor, I need a complete physical exam. I want to know if something is wrong."

The doctor shook his head. "Lady," he told her, "You look pretty healthy to me. At first glance I see only a couple of things wrong with you. For one, your slip is showing; and, secondly, you need glasses. Further, the sign on my door says, 'Dr. O'Brien - Veterinarian'."

****

Today it costs about forty bucks when a physician paints your sore throat. Many folks can remember when you could get your house painted for that.

****

"One thing sure," the doctor told his patient, "Your pulse is steady as a clock."

"No wonder! You got your fingers on my wristwatch."

****

"Howdy, Mary, how is your son, the physician?"

"Just fine. But he had to quit practicing obstetrics."

"Really? Why?"

"As you know, he worked his way through medical school with a job in the post office. Well, he just could not overcome the one very bad habit he learned there."

"Oh my goodness! What was the problem?"

"It took him six weeks to deliver a baby!"

****

"Doc, what's the difference between a psychiatrist and a psychologist?"

"A psychologist is a blind man in a pitch black attic looking for a black cat. A psychiatrist is a blind man in a pitch black attic looking for a black cat that isn't there."

****

Two psychiatrists met on the street one late afternoon. The younger doctor said, "George, I don't how you do it, a man your age! Here you are looking like you were just starting out. How can you look so fresh after listening to patients complain all day?"

The elder doctor replied: "Who listens?"

"Doctor, can you explain to me the difference between a neurotic and a psychotic?"

"I'll try. You see, a neurotic builds castles in the air. A psychotic actually lives in those castles and a psychiatrist attempts to treat them both..."

"Yeah? How?"

"He collects the rent!"

****

During World War II, a citizen was summoned for military service. He faced the army ophthalmologist who asked him to read a chart.

"I don't see any chart," the draftee replied. "Where?"

"Just sit down in that chair and we'll proceed," the doctor said.

"What chair?" responded the draftee.

His responses got him a deferment. Delighted, the man went to a nearby movie and, when the lights came on, he was petrified to discover that the ophthalmologist was seated next to him.

"Pardon me, Sir," the conscript said, "does this bus go to Petersburg?"

****

Many doctors believe in the efficiency of shock treatment -- mailed the first of the month.

****

Americans love these wild exaggerations and here is a prime example of the tall tale genre.

Two friends were walking down a county road and the one was complaining about his bad eyesight. To test him, the friend asked if he could see the barn over at the end of the adjacent cornfield. "Not very clearly, Fred, it's real hazy."

"Well, there is a beetle crawling on the roof, you know. Interesting specimen."

"Yes, yes. I know that."

"You do? But you can't see the barn, let alone the beetle! How come?"

"True, I sure can't see that barn. But I can hear the shingles crack every time one of those beetles crawls around."

****

Have you ever noticed how much more readable is the doctor's bill than his handwriting?

What we see with the eye is impressed upon us, our memory, more than what we hear with the ear. Ophthalmologists know that. For example, two spinsters heard the drone of an overhead aeroplane. They looked up and the one spinster remarked, "It's a mail plane."

The other spinster said, "My goodness, but you have good eyesight."

****

That same lady then told her friend that she had mistakenly gone to a house where a nude party was in progress. "And a nude butler answered my ring!" she said.

"Just how the heck did you know he was the butler...in the nude and all?"

"Well, gosh, it sure wasn't the maid!"

****

A psychiatrist was examining a country patient, a farmer who seemed not overburdened with "the smarts." He began to ask questions. "What's the opposite of sorrow?"

"Easy, Doc...joy."

"And the opposite of misery?"

"Even easier, Doc...happiness."

The physician was surprised and pleased. "You're doing great. Now tell me the opposite of woe."

"Giddyap!"

****

"Dim your brights, I can't see where I'm going."

Don Herold was the beloved humorist of the early part of this century. In 1926, he wrote *There Ought To Be A Law,* in which he described the new trend in medicine toward specialization. One wonders what he would have to say today, given the specialized condition of the medical profession. Perhaps the reader can get an answer to that question from this excerpt:

Specialists, Specialists Everywhere
But Not a Doctor in Sight

Who remembers when we used to call a doctor in case of sickness?

Nowadays, we have to be mighty delicate about that. We might get an inch over the boundary line and call a doctor for the wrong organ. Lots of people just die now rather than try to decide which specialist to summon.

In the big cities, at any rate, there is nobody to come and see us when we are just sick. We have to know exactly where we are sick and what ails us.

Half the time we are sick in between organs, so there is nobody in town to cover the situation. The only thing to do is to wait until the disease shifts to some part of our anatomy covered by a specialist of whom we happen to know.

What is needed is a medical brokerage service. When theaters became so numerous in New York, for example, that it was impossible to run around to all of them to decide what show to see, ticket agencies naturally sprung up where you could stand in front of a counter and get a seat for any show in town. We need McBrides and Tysons for the medical profession. We need medical brokers who will send us where we belong.

Once there used to be a few accepted kinds of specialists--ear, nose and throat men, for instance. Why, gosh, a man who covers the ear, nose and throat today is almost a general practitioner. There are now twenty-seven kinds of nose doctors alone. A man can now devote his whole life to the outside of the inside ear.

Back in Bloomfield the same doctor used to bring us and bury us. Here in New York, the obstetrician gives us a slap and a promise and turns us over to the pediatrician. There is a new doctor down the line every fifteen or twenty minutes from the cradle to the grave. People are not only chopped up into sections geographically but chronologically.

A liver man will not even listen to your lungs. A heart man does not care how you are--all he knows about is hearts. And practically none of the new-fashioned doctors cares how you feel.

Let us pray that this intense specialization does not spread to other fields. It may be well and good to peddle a stomach-ache all over Manhattan before finding a buyer, but may we be spared from dragging a motor car all over the city to find "the right man."

"Oh, now, we don't touch that. You will have to take your car to a rear axle specialist. We concentrate on these teeny weeny little wires in your spark plugs. And for that hoarseness in your klaxon, you should see Croupem, the horn man."

****

Cowgirl at the gynecologist's office: "Doc, I feel like I been rode hard and put up wet!"

****

They tell the story of a physically powerful M.D., nearly seven feet tall and weighing over three hundred pounds! And he had a miserable disposition, lorded it over the other physicians in his group, was an absolute pain in the neck. And the most offensive characteristic was his conceit! He knew it all.

When the giant died, they couldn't find a coffin huge enough to contain this enormous M.D. They shopped all over the state. No luck at all. Finally, they held a conference, devised a method, gave the giant an enema and buried him in a shoebox!

****

"Forget getting your fee from him...he's too poor to paint and too proud to whitewash."

****

Here's one about a psychiatrist who was gifted with unimpeachable logic.

A woman came to see him and complained, "Doctor, I have a terrible problem. I have thirteen kids and I just discovered I'm not compatible with my husband."

"Madam," the doctor responded. "Take heart. Just imagine your condition if you were."

****

Has the near-universal use of "the pill" made the stork one of our endangered species?

****

Doctor: "I must tell you, Mr. Roberts, that the best thing for you is to give up wine, women and song."

Patient: "That so? Well what's the next best thing?"

35

A Wisconsin ophthalmologist prescribed glasses for a farmer who later sent him this note:

Friend Doctor. I thought I'd drop you a line on those new bifocals you gave me. Since wearing them, I have...

Fallen down the stairs.

Haltingly stumbled upstairs.

Amputated the right fender of the family Ford.

Given the barber a tip of a silver dollar instead of a quarter.

Missed sinking six foot putts at a buck a putt.

Badly bit my right hand thumb while trying to feed myself a hot dog.

Nicked the wife's ear, instead of her lips.

I was wondering if you could make me a simple set, something in country-style, a pair of unifocals, something simple like a bamboo rod, line and hook kind of thing that'd let me get out from back of these absolutely useless if scientifically correct spellbinders.

Rather shakily, even dazedly yours.......

****

Suggested advertisement for an obstetrician, "Pay as you grow."

Suggested advertisement for a maternity shop: "We provide the accessories after the fact."

****

Definition of a physician: A person who poses as a humanitarian and charges like a plumber.

****

Then there was the truly grateful patient who gushed to the doctor these words of appreciation: "Doctor, dear Doctor, how can I ever repay you?"

The doctor replied, "By check, money order or cash."

****

Dr. Mary Parsimony was walking leisurely down the street toward her office when a smart-aleck-wolf sidled up to her and said, "Howdy, Babe, what's doin' just now?" But Dr. Parsimony said not a word, merely turned her head and gave him a ferocious scowl.

"Pardon me all...to...hell," the would-be wolf snapped, "but I thought you were my mother."

"Impossible," rejoined Dr. Parsimony, "I'm married."

Then there's the old saw about the man who visited a psychiatrist and complained of constantly thinking of himself as a dog. "How long has this been going on?" the psychiatrist asked. "Since I was a puppy," was the reply.

****

According to the magazines in my doctor's office, business will boom in 1970 and 1980 promises to be even better.

****

Doctors recommend laughter as a tranquilizer with no side effects.

****

A physician who notoriously underpaid his staff was known as a man with short arms and long pockets.

****

Doctor: "What is your maximum weight?"
Patient: "One hundred and fifty pounds."
Doctor: "And the least you ever weighed?"
Patient: "Seven and a half pounds."

****

If you want free advice (whoops -- that should be *fee* advice), go to a physician or lawyer.

****

A man went to the psychiatrist complaining of his feelings of inferiority about being so short. The psychiatrist reassured him that many men of short stature in history became great like Napoleon, Henry the VIII, Toulouse Lautrec, etc.
The little guy felt great after the talk. Everything would have been just fine, except that a cat ate him.

****

If you want to study ancient history, just go to a doctor's waiting room and read!

A psychiatrist's analysis of the world:

There was a psychiatrist from Cadiz
Who concluded life is what it is.
For she early had learnt
If it were what it weren't
It could not be that which it is.

****

That same psychiatrist might have penned this obituary:

Here lies a woman of pious worth;
Who always wished she'd have the earth.

And now at last she's really found it;
She's got the earth...with a fence around it!

****

On their rare-enough night out, three plastic surgeons were boasting about their most significant accomplishments. One physician began, "I grafted a leg on a man and he later became a champion cross-country runner."

"That's pretty good, but I did something more professional. I grafted an arm on a patient and he later became a champion golfer."

The third doctor, a bit put off by all this, said, "I got you guys beat all to hell! I grafted a smile on a jackass and he later became a U.S. Senator!"

****

It is foolish to argue with your physician because he has inside information.

****

In a spirit of levity, the professors at a certain medical school decided to confer a Ph.D. on a wonderful horse that had been used in innumerable experiments resulting in good to humanity. At the celebration, the head of the medical school arose to address the assembled fun-makers. "Honored guests and friends of the horse we are about to honor with a Ph.D.....a doctor of Posterior Horse. It is a precedent-breaking thing that we do. But I must tell you...this is the first time that I have awarded a degree to an *entire, a whole horse*!"

"DO I WANT TO PLAY DOCTOR? SURE — I'LL BE
YOUR MALPRACTICE ATTORNEY."

****

An investigative reporter was given the job of examining the claims -- made by various American companies -- to enhance the health of Americans. The business of health is one of billions of dollars annually.

He directed an inquiry to a Burlington, Iowa physician concerning claims made by a certain candy company preferred by physicians - especially their brand -- Dandy Candy.

The doctor's reply was: "I can tell you honestly that all the doctors I know, without exception, prefer women."

****

"They say time heals all things," the old lady remarked to her neighbor. "But I can tell you one thing, time sure ain't no beauty specialist."

****

Have you heard of the new Oriental system for weight reduction? It makes a lot of sense. You eat for an hour but you only use one chop stick.

Definition of a proctologist: A superduper poopersnooper.

****

An actor complained about constant ringing in his ears. His doctor recommended having his tonsils out. He did. But that didn't help. So he went to another physician who recommended having his teeth pulled. This he did but without even the slightest diminution in that awful ringing in his ears. A third doctor told him to quit eating meat, to become a vegetarian. He did this for six months, but got no relief.

The guy was ready to end his life! But first he wanted to take a long vacation and to buy himself the very best clothing for the trip. He ordered a bunch of suits, shoes, sox, etc. Then he went to a shirtmaker and ordered fifty shirts, sleeve, thirty-three and collar, fifteen. The shirtmaker insisted on measuring the man and stated, "Sir, you measure sixteen around the neck, not fifteen."

"That can't be right," the actor shouted, "I've always worn a fifteen shirt...all my life and that's what I want."

"Well, Sir, it's your business and we'll make them size fifteen. But I tell you this, you're gonna get the goshawfulest ringing in your ears!"

****

A well-known physician at the Mayo Clinic has this sign on his desk: "A sense of humor is what makes you laugh at something that would make you furious if it happened to you."

****

The medical profession is doing research on laziness, trying to eliminate it. Isn't it a crying shame? Someone is always trying to take the joy out of life.

****

"How's your practice, Doctor?"

"Lousy. Not nearly as good as last year. I had lots more patients then."

"Wonder what happened to them, Doctor?"

"We can only hope for the best."

****

Old Doc Patton is just too darned tight. What a cheapee. He makes a nickel go so far the buffalo gets sore feet.

40

"THEY SAY INSIDE EVERY FAT PERSON THERE'S
A THIN PERSON TRYING TO GET OUT—ACCORDING
TO MY TESTS, THOUGH, YOU HAVE TWO."

****

"A cold is both positive and negative: sometimes the EYES have it and sometimes the NOSE." William Lyon Phelps.

****

"Don't you know that my office hours are from two to five afternoons?"
Caller: "I sure do, Doc. But the car that hit me didn't."

****

One of the best ways to cure a woman of nerves is to tell her it is caused by advancing age!

****

"I can't *make* you lose weight, Mrs. Tompkins," the doctor told her. "Just remember that it's two minutes in the mouth, two hours in the stomach and a lifetime on the hips."

A physician charged with using profanity to a nurse, was brought before a Board of Inquiry.

"Did you shout obscenities at this nurse?" a board member asked.

"Let me explain!" the physician replied. "The alarm went off this morning and I got up to stop it. I tripped on the rug, fell and broke the lamp, bruising my head. Then, as I was shaving, the doorbell rang and I was so startled that I cut myself. I went to the door where a young fellow tried to sell me kitchen utensils and I had to buy six to get rid of him. By then the toast was burnt, the coffee cold, so I started to get in the car to drive here and caught my pocket on the door handle and tearing my pants. Then the car wouldn't start. I called the garage and waited an hour for a man to come out and fix it. After fixing, I got in and drove here to the hospital and, as I pulled in the driveway, a taxi hit me and it'll cost me $5,000 for repairs. Well, when I finally got to the office, hours later, the nurse who complained about my using profanity came to my office and asked, 'Doctor, I just received two dozen thermometers. What shall I do with them?'

"So, I told her."

****

Some doctors are brave enough to tell their patients the bad news face-to-face. But others prefer to mail the bill!

****

Doctor Edgar Daniels was driving on a curving country road when he ran smack-dab into another car. The other driver exchanged necessary information concerning insurance, etc. After a bit, Dr. Daniels reached into his car and took out a flask, saying, "You seem a bit nervous, fellow. I'm a physician and I recommend that you take a swig of this to steady your nerves."

The other fellow took a big swig, then handed the bottle to Dr. Daniels who put it back in his car. "Aren't you going to have a drink, too, to steady yourself?" the other man asked.

"In a bit. After the police get here."

****

The doctor completed a thorough physical examination of the 100-year-old man. "Astonishing," the doctor said, "that you should reach such an advanced age and be in such good, even great health. What is your notion of how you've been able to live so well this long?"

"Ain't a lot to it," the old man replied. "You just gotta keep breathin'."

42

The same fellow reached 101 years and came home one evening to discover all the neighbors and a newspaper reporter gathered at his home to honor him. "Sir, you sure do look mighty vigorous," the reporter told him. "Can you still get out and walk as well as you could ten years ago?"

"Let me put her thisaway, young feller...I can walk a heluva lot better than I could 101 years ago!"

****

An obstetrician from Texas was bragging about the big baby he had recently delivered, down in Pyote, Texas. "Why, they had to use sheets 81" wide and 152" long. Kids grow big in Texas, all right, but I never delivered one as big as that one was. Whew!"

"Hey, man!" jeered his classmate from New Mexico. "That's not such a big baby. Out in my state, that's standard size for our babies."

"For diapers?" the Texas physician asked.

****

They tell of a doctor who became insane and turned to kidnapping. But he was highly unsuccessful: his ransom notes were unreadable.

****

Her children brought the Widow Gonzales to the psychiatrist for advice on how to help her recover from the recent death of her husband.

"Perhaps it would be good to talk a bit about his death," the doctor suggested. "Why not tell me how he died."

"He was keeled by a weasel," the widow sobbed.

"By a weasel? Perhaps rabies? Blood poisoning? I'm not sure I understand."

"No! No!" the widow replied. "He was keeled by a weasel. The train come and Pedro he no hear da weasel."

****

Then there is the story, told as true many years ago, about the business tycoon who was hospitalized for several weeks. He was so well taken care of by one particular orderly that, when he finally checked out of the hospital, he gave him a huge gratuity and complimented him before the staff and nurses. The orderly was overwhelmed by these favors and said, "By gosh, Sir, we sure are gonna miss ya around here. You sure did take a mighty good enema."

There are certain telling phrases used to describe the feelings of a young medical student about to begin the first major operation surrounded by his professors, fellow students and all. Some of these phrases follow:

"He was as nervous as a bastard at a family reunion."
"Nervous? You bet! As nervous as a whore in church!"

"Was I nervous? You shouldn't ask: Why, man, I was as nervous as a long-tailed cat in a room full of rocking chairs! "

****

After six years in a mental institution, the patient had been pronounced sane and was permitted to go out into the world. But the social worker was a bit worried and asked him just what he intended to do to earn a living.

"That's easy," said the former patient. I could go into law since I have a law degree and can surely pass the bar exam.

"Gee, that's great," the social worker exclaimed.

"Or...I might go into business. I'm a C.P.A., you know."

"No, I didn't know. That's just fine."

"Or I could go back to my former practice of medicine. I've an M.D. degree and, since I've been here I've read up on Freud, Adler, Jung, Watson, Kempf, Berman and many more."

"Well, we for sure don't have to worry about you, Doctor. You'll get along great."

"What's more," the former patient declared, "If none of that pans out, well, I can always be a coffee pot."

****

A laugh is worth more than a hundred groans in any market.

****

A maiden at college, Ms. Eves,
Had too many B.A.'s and Lit D's.
She collapsed from the strain,
Said her doctor, "It's plain,
You are killing yourself by degrees."

****

"Doctor, I'm feeling, mighty puny...like I got one foot in the grave and the other on a banana peel."

They tell the story about a visit the governor of New Jersey made to a state mental institution. It was a Saturday night and the patients were all gussied up in suits and cute dresses, ready for a dandy evening. But the sexes were segregated and the governor asked why.

A psychiatrist answered: "They aren't *that* crazy!"

****

Doctor: "You tell me that your son spends hours making mud pies. Well, I don't think that's so serious. I wouldn't worry about it!"

Patient: "Well, Doctor, I do worry. I worry a lot about it. And so does his wife."

****

Doctor: "Sir, could you pay for an operation if I thought one was required?"

Patient: "Would you think one was required if I couldn't pay for it?"

****

"Whoops!" exclaimed the surgeon as he dropped the forceps. "Those blamed things are slipperier than a pocket full of custard."

****

Doctors and lawyers don't often find themselves in agreement. But they do agree that the best things in life are fee.

****

A restaurant on Sixth Avenue offered a wide range of breakfast selections. As the doctor perused the menu, he noticed his waiter was continually scratching his rear end. "I wonder if you have hemorrhoids?" the doctor whispered. "Naw, Sir," the waiter responded, "We don't allow no substitutions on dat breakfast menu."

****

There was a time when two people could talk about their problems over coffee and a cigarette. But now, those two things are the problem.

In World War II, they told the story of two draftees standing before the medical examiner's tent, awaiting their physical examination. The one lad went in for his exam, then came out grinning. "Did they accept you?" his friend asked. "Nope, I've worn a truss for ten years so they rejected me."

"Lend it to me, will you?"

"Sure," said the friend, handing it over.

When the faker got inside, the doctor asked him how long he'd worn the truss. The doctor looked him over, examined him up and drown, then wrote in his record, *M.E.*

"What does that *M.E.* mean, Doctor?" the draftee asked.

"It means Middle East. Anyone who can wear a double truss upside down for twelve years can easily ride a camel. You're in, buddy!"

****

Many readers will remember Bob Burns, the comedian who told about his Uncle Hy Drangia, who became a doctor by taking correspondence courses. Yep. His major problem as a diagnostician was that he was too dadblamed absent-minded. For example, every time he read a book, he removed its appendix.

And his handwriting wasn't so good either. Once he wrote a prescription for Grandpa Snazzy that was so illegible that Grandpa not only got his medicine at the drugstore but the prescription slip served Grandpa as a pass on the railroads, got him into an unlimited number of picture shows and ball-games free. Not only that, but his daughter used it on their player piano.

****

Laughter is the shock absorber that cushions the blows of life.

****

Dr. Mary Jordan was flying from her hometown to New York when a stewardess approached her. "Doctor," she said, "You'll be pleased to know that this is the first all-woman flight. Both pilot and co-pilot are women as are all the flight attendants."

"Why, that's simply marvelous," enthused Dr. Jordan, herself a rabid feminist. "Before we land, I must go and meet them. I'd like to thank everyone in the cockpit."

"Begging your pardon, Doctor, but we don't call it that anymore."

" THIS SIDE EFFECT, MR HINKLE, IS THE ONE I NEGLECTED TO MENTION."

****

Here are some telling definitions submitted by a freshman chemistry class:

Chlorine: A dancer in a night club.
Atimony: A fee that ex-wives collect from former husbands they were smart enough to leave.
Carbon: A big building for storing cars.
Barium: What the undertaker does with dead folks.
Catalyst: A guy who works on a western ranch.
Boron: A person of extremely low mentality.
Electrolyte: A contrivance that, when it's dark, you turn it on to get things bright.
Atom: Eve's mate.
Tension: What the officer demands of his troops.
Lattice: A vegetable.
Miscible: Dissatisfied...unhappy.
Fehling: Below the passing mark on the final exam.
Tin: Not fat.

"Howdy, Doc, I'm sure glad to see you. I called last month but you were on vacation."

"Yes'm. I took a vacation in Canada. Went hunting."

"Any luck? Bag anything? Moose? Deer? Bear?"

"Heck no. Didn't fire a shot. Why we didn't hardly kill any wild game at all..."

"Hey, that's sure a shame, Doc. Heck fire...you could have scored a lot better'n that just stayin' home and lookin' after your practice."

****

"George, do you know Doctor Hugh Edwards?"

"Of course. First rate surgeon. I never understood why he retired so young. Couldn't have been more than forty."

"Forty-two. But he sure was too young to retire. You know, he had this odd habit that he couldn't get rid of. Tried everything...psychiatry, psychology, religion...nothing helped."

"Goodness. That must have been a perfectly terrible habit that it could cause him to retire. Do you know what it was?"

"Yep. He couldn't quit humming while he worked with patients. He just hummed that same old tune over and over...'Nearer My God to Thee'."

****

A psychiatrist once remarked that his experience had shown that an optimist sees the donut, the pessimist sees the hole, and the realist sees the calories.

****

Samuel Johnson (1709-1784), the revered political philosopher and man of letters, once remarked: "My diseases are an asthma and a dropsy and, what is less curable, seventy-five."

****

A man came in to his doctor for a premarital blood test prior to his second marriage.

The doctor was a bit rough on him. "Your wife's been dead only two months and now you tell me you plan to marry next month. Couldn't you have waited?"

"Hey, Doc, let me tell ya...I'm the kind of guy who don't hold a grudge long."

You don't have to be a physician to know that the severity of an itch is inversely proportionate to the reach.

****

"It's hard to squelch an American," the physician told a friend. "I had a patient who was near death. So I told him that one more clean shirt would do him. And he replied, 'Yeah, Doc, that ain't such good news. But, on the other hand, look at all the laundry money I'll save.'"

****

Bob Hope used to tell this story as he entertained American troops during World War II. It seems that an English doctor was examining the charts in an American base hospital. He noted that S.F. meant Scarlet Fever and T.B. stood for Tuberculosis. But he could not understand one abbreviation: G.O.K. "What does this mean? This G.O.K.?" he asked.
"Oh, that? Well, when we don't know what the hell's the matter we write G.O.K. It stands for God Only Knows."

****

The attending physician turned to the young intern who was working with him and snarled: "When I want your opinion, I'll give it to you."

****

It is said that every physician should have this glossary:

Alcoholic:	A sufferer from Bourbonic plague, or Scotchtapeworm.
Bachelor:	A gentleman who has no kids...to speak of.
Bald head:	A time or condition when there shall be no more parting, neither shall there be dyeing.
Birth:	Known as Commencement Day.
Buck Fever:	An incessant craving for dollar bills.
Champagne:	A feigned illness, a sham.
Chiropractor:	One who kneads patients.
College Graduate:	One who can count to twenty without removing his shoes.
Diet:	Triumph of mind over platter.

Three European doctors were discussing the plight of a couple who were childless. It was rumored that the woman was sterile. They struggled with the English language in order to express the problem.

"The wife is simply unbearable," the foreign doctor said.

"You haven't quite the right word, my friend," said the second doctor. "What you mean to say is that she is...is...inconceivable."

"Both of you are wrong," said the third foreign doctor. "You should have said that she is...impregnable."

****

"I'm eighty in two weeks, Doctor," the old fellow said. "I can't believe it."

"I know what you mean," the doctor replied. "Birthdays are like underwear shorts...they creep up on you."

****

"If you are uncomfortable with that excess fat of yours," the doctor said, "I suggest you wear a girdle...a device that'll keep an unfortunate condition from spreading."

****

A medical student was leaving the library where she'd been checking vital statistics for a research paper. She met a friend and said, "This has been some experience. Hard to realize how many young people die every minute. Why, every time I breathe somebody dies."

"Why don't you try Lavoris or Listerine," her friend replied.

****

A doctor fell into a well,
And broke his collar bone.
A doctor should attend the sick,
And leave the well alone.

****

"Of course, I've been following your suggestion on sea food," the patient told his doctor. "Whenever I see food, I eat it."

****

Dr. Peter Fredericks had attended his fortieth class reunion. When asked how it had gone with him, he said, "A class reunion is where we come together to see who's falling apart."

The psychiatrist had listened to the sad words of the couple whose marriage was falling apart. "You tend to blame parents on both sides for your trouble," the doctor said. "Just remember that it wasn't the apple in the tree that caused the trouble in Eden...it was the pair on the ground."

****

"I've discovered the meaning of true happiness," the patient said after completing her 14-day diet. "Happiness is the fifteenth day!"

****

The biology instructor was "fed up" with his students coming to class with mouths filled with chewing gum. Finally he read them this poem:

> Gum-chewing students and cud-chewing cows
> There may be a difference, you've got to allow;
> It's not what they chew or even how,
> But the intelligent look on the face of the cow.

****

A famous dermatologist penned this free diagnosis: "If your palm itches, you're about to get something. If your scalp itches...you've got it."

****

A physician was out hunting quail when, one cold November day, a nude blonde flashed by running like crazy. She was followed by two men chasing her and a third holding a pail of sand.

"What's going on?" yelled the doctor.

"We got to catch that girl. She escaped from the Psychiatric Zone Center," the pail-carrier panted as he ran along.

"What are you doing with that pail of sand?" the doctor called after him.

"That's my handicap," the pail-carrier called back. "I caught her yesterday."

****

Patient's question: "If exercise does so darned much good for people, how come athletes retire at 35?"

51

A patient complained to her physician of a constant, prolonged headache.

"Quit smoking at once," the physician told her.

"But, Doctor, I don't smoke."

"Then quit drinking."

"But I don't drink at all, Doctor."

"Then lay off the men."

"But I'm a virgin, Doctor...always in bed by nine thirty. Alone."

"Then I suggest you go to the store and get a new halo. Yours is too tight."

****

It was final exam time for the medical students and one of them was really puzzled by a question:

"Name six advantages to mother's milk over cow's or goat's milk, or manufactured milk." He thought awhile, then gave these answers:

1. It is almost always available when and where needed.
2. You can count on its freshness.
3. It is always sanitary, pure.
4. The temperature is as prescribed.
5. No cat or other animal can contaminate it.
6. It comes in incomparably cute containers.

****

Here's one doctors tell about themselves. Dr. Homer P. Newell, M.D. pulled this 'un:

A man is informed, after a thorough operation, that he will need an entire brain transplant.

"Oh, my gosh. Well," says the patient, "How much will all that cost?"

"Depends on whose brains you use, Sir," the doctor replied. "Select a policeman's brains and it'll cost you five bucks an ounce. But a stockbroker's brains'll cost one hundred dollars an ounce. However, you can select a dermatologist's brains, if you wish, at a cost of one...thousand...dollars an ounce."

"But why should a dermatologist's brain cost so darned much? And I always wanted to be a dermatologist. Why so high?"

"Have you any notion, any idea at all, how many dermatologists it takes to get an ounce of brain?" was the reply.

****

"If we are what we eat, I'm worried," the patient said.

"Why is that?" the physician asked.

"Well you see...I snack on nuts."

Physicians get a lot of strange replies when they ask patients to describe their symptoms. Here are a few:

"Doc, I got the wigglies."

"Doc, I've been sittin' on the anxious seat for weeks and weeks."

"Doc, I'm nervous all the time, nervous as an old maid in an asparagus patch."

"Doc, I'm jumpy as a cricket on a hot stove."

"Doc, I'm nervous as a porcupine in a balloon factory."

****

The one thing that plastic surgeons have not been able to do with a nose job is to keep it out of other people's business.

****

When Doctor William Caldwell's car wouldn't start, he was forced to take the subway to his Manhattan office. The train was terribly crowded and he had to stand. But the obese woman in front of him insisted on shoving her feet back and forth on top of his. So crowded was it that there was no way to avoid her constant shifting.

"Madam," he said politely, "I'd sure appreciate it if you'd backtrack a bit and keep off my foot."

"Mister," she exploded, "you put your damned feet where they belong."

"Don't tempt me," Dr. Caldwell replied. "Just...don't...tempt...me."

****

It is rumored in veterinary circles that an owl with laryngitis, doesn't give a hoot.

****

There's an old proverb that advises: Don't smoke in bed. The ashes on the floor may be you.

****

There are some people you just can't please. Consider the situation of this sweet old lady who passed on and got to heaven. Six years later, her beloved husband died and was reunited with her up there. Well, the old girl could hardly wait to show him all the beautiful places in heaven. They had a grand old time heaven-seeing.

"You are absolutely right, dear," the old man told her. "This is a truly beautiful place...and if it weren't for that dadblasted fibre diet of yours, I could have been up here enjoying things years ago! "

"I don't think he's been practicing medicine very long. These magazines are all new!"

****

MORE MEDICAL TERMS

Halitosis:	A breath that takes yours away.
Hypochondriac:	One who is happy being miserable.
Nurse:	A pan handler.
Obesity:	Surplus gone to waist.
Papoose:	The consolation an Indian brave gets for taking a chance on an Indian blanket.
Paradox:	A vision of two physicians.
Party:	A place where you can always find room for one more.
Pretzel:	A biscuit with rickets.
Psychiatrist (in the South):	One who likes Freud chicken.
Stork:	A bird whose bill rivals the obstetrician's.

****

Definition of a contraceptive: A bit of apparel that one should wear on every conceivable occasion.

The old man went to the dermatologist to see about getting some help with his falling hair. The physician examined him and said, "Sir, there are three problems with hair like yours. If *parted*, I can help. If *unparted*, I can help. But if *departed*, I can be of no help at all."

****

Old Doc Foster has a unique and effective way for patients to get the most good out of a diet. He has them place their bathroom scale in front of the refrigerator.

****

"I admire a man who holds his head high," the doctor said. "But I'm never sure as to whether he is a proud soul or in need of bifocals."

****

One measure of your age is to observe your workouts. If what you once did for a warm-up is now a humongous workout, you're getting up there.

****

"Doctor, I'm constantly being embarrassed by my faulty memory. I forget everything."
"Perhaps I can help you," the doctor said. "Let's get to first things first."
"What do you mean, Doctor?"
"Pay me now."

****

The woman entered a small room off the hotel lobby, and was surprised to see her physician, Dr. Joe Cutup pacing up and down.
"Why, Doctor...what are you doing here?"
"I'm about to make a speech."
"Does it make you so nervous as all that?"
"Nervous? What do you mean?"
"Well, Doctor, you know it is kind of unusual to see you in the ladies restroom."

****

An obstetrician has been defined as a delivery man who relies on the stork market.

The physician laid down the law to his elderly, philandering patient. "Wine and women are out for you. But from now on you can, in moderation, sing."

****

After many months of repeated billing, the doctor wrote his deadbeat patient a note. "Sir, would you please delegate me as a pallbearer at your funeral. It seems only fair that since I've carried you this far I continue on and finish the job."

****

Dr. Edward Pierson has a sign that stands high on the back of the magazine table in his reception room. It reads, "ENJOY LIFE -- THIS IS NOT A DRESS REHEARSAL."

****

"My patient in 531 has become so skinny that I've had to put him on skis to keep him from slipping down the drain."

****

It is said that a student who hoped to specialize in obstetrics composed this poem:
> The bee is such a busy soul,
> It has no time for birth control.
> And that is why, in times like these,
> There are so many sons of bees.

****

A doctor on his way to the hospital had a flat tire just outside a mental institution. He got out of the car and removed the flat tire, but the bolts from the rim rolled down the sewer. He stood there wondering what to do.

A voice came from the window of the institution. "Take one bolt off each of the other tires to hold that wheel in place until you get to a gas station."

"Thanks a million, Sir. That was brilliant. I don't know why they have you in there..."

"I'm crazy...not stupid."

****

People with laryngitis sure don't talk much about it.

Two women were in the maternity ward, each having been delivered of a child. The one mother said, "I have six boys."

The other woman, whose bed was adjacent, said, "I sure as heck wish I had six kids."

"Don't you have any except the one you just had?"

"Yeah. Ten."

****

The country doctor retired after fifty years of community service. A reporter for the local newspaper was sent to interview him. Among the questions, the reporter asked if he had advice to give younger colleagues. "I would advise," said the old doctor, "that they follow what Mark Twain advised long ago...'Never put off till tomorrow what you can just as well do the day after.'"

****

The lady went to her doctor to discover what he could recommend for her to lose weight. The doctor went to his medical cabinet and removed a large bottle of pills. "Now these pills you don't take orally," he said, "but you do spill them on the floor, then pick them up and put them back in the bottle, one by one, and you do this three times a day. Guaranteed to make you lose weight."

****

It may be true that the physician of long ago didn't know exactly what was wrong with you, but there's one thing sure...he didn't charge you fifty bucks to send you to a doctor who did.

****

"Please, Doctor, help my husband. He thinks that he is a parking meter and neither I nor anyone else can talk him out of it."

"Are you sure you've done all you can to cure him of this obsession?"

"Yes, I have. I'm at my wit's end. The trouble is, he won't talk."

"Why not?"

"How can he with his mouth full of coins?"

****

Lawyers are great,
So are physicians.
But I'd sure die,
Before I called a mortician.

And yet another case of delusion. It seems that a husband went to his doctor and complained that his wife of thirty years had, for a year, thought of herself as a lawnmower.

"My that is odd," the psychiatrist said. "But tell me, Sir, why have you waited for a year to come tell me about this?"

"I couldn't come sooner, Doc, because my neighbor just brought her back."

****

You know you are middle aged when your wife tells you to pull in your belly and you already have.

****

"The solution to your plumpness is threefold; remove the narcissus complex that is disturbing you, bring your psyche in harmony with your libido, and stop eating like a horse."

(Reprinted from The Saturday Evening Post)

****

There is one way to ascertain whether an alcoholic is recovering or not. Watch him when he takes his medicine. If he doesn't try to blow the foam off, he's on his way.

"Howdy do, Doctor. I've come to see you because my wife insists that I do."

"Fine. Just what does she think is wrong with you?"

"Well, you see...I prefer loafers to standard, laced oxfords."

"Nothing erratic about that. I prefer them myself."

"Oh, good! But tell me, Doctor, do you like yours fried or broiled with garlic?"

****

Another case of obsession refers to a woman who rushed into the doctor's office begging for help. "What is the trouble, Madam?" the doctor asked.

"It's my husband," she cried. "It's so awful. He thinks he's a chicken."

"That is awful," the doctor agreed. "Bring him in and let me see him."

"Oh, I can't do that, Doctor. We desperately need the eggs."

****

"One thing about the past that you say I'm living in," the patient said to the psychiatrist, "It's a damned sight cheaper."

****

Dr. Peter Levy practiced medicine in a small, impoverished community near a coal mine, which was the principal source of income for the community. Many patients never paid him, but he treated them all, anyway. Then, one day, a patient whom he had been treating for a year came into the office and he informed her that she was now fine, perfectly well. "Oh, Doctor," she exclaimed. "I'm so happy. What can I do to show my appreciation?"

"Madam, ever since the Phoenicians invented money," the doctor began, "the answer to that question has been obvious."

****

Old Jed Robinson had been a heavy drinker for years. At last, the doctor told him he must not have more than one drink a day. So far, Jed is up to March 21, 1998.

****

Psychiatrist: "If I understand you correctly, Sir, your problem is that you have trouble making up your mind."

Patient: "Well, Doctor...yes and no."

A man had a serious problem with his bladder. He could not contain, hold his urine. He went to his doctor who gave him this advice. "My suggestion is that you go to a psychiatrist. That'll cost you seventy-five dollars a visit."

"Doctor, I can't afford that. Is there anything else I could do?"

"Yes, there is. You can buy rubber shorts at five dollars a pair."

****

A pediatrician pronounced this wise observation: "Far more ominous that the sound of a riot is to hear a bunch of kids go suddenly quiet."

****

While it is not common knowledge, the rumor is going around that at Washington Street Hospital, in Springfield, Illinois, the Hippocratic Oath that all doctors must take before licensing, is actually an oath against poverty.

****

Dr. Hugh Graham was invited to address a junior high school on the subject of premarital sex. He informed his wife but was a bit embarrassed and, instead of telling her the true subject, he said he was going to talk to the kids about sailing.

A few days after his lecture to the kids, his wife met the school principal who remarked, "Your husband was just great. The kids really learned a lot and were very impressed."

"Now that does surprise me," the doctor's wife said, "because, so far as I know, he's only done it twice. The first time he got terribly sick and puked all over the bed...and the second time, he lost his hat."

****

Dr. Mabel Long was talking to her associate, Dr. George Caldwell. "Tell me, Dr. Caldwell," she asked, "Are you finally reconciled to the need of women to fight for their rights?"

"By all means, yes. With one proviso. That it is the woman, more than the rights, that need redressing."

****

"Mr. Smith." the doctor advised his down-in-the-dumps patient, "Quit worrying so much. Worry is kinda like a rocking chair...it gives you something to do but sure doesn't get you anywhere."

60

A professor at a midwestern medical school loves to tell tall tales. He once regaled his students with the case of a young boy who grew so fast that his shadow couldn't keep pace with him. That boy grew and grew until he had to get on a chair to button his collar. Some months later, when his head had grown through the top of his hat, his doctor said, "Son, you'll have to eat lard."

"But why lard?" the kid asked.

"It's time for shortening," was the reply.

****

If you enter a doctor's office and notice that all of his plants are dead...get the heck out of there!

****

There was an indigent young Dr.
Called in by a woman named Prr.
    With a battery he shr,
    Quite senseless he kntr,
Ten plunks was the sum that he sktr.

****

"But you told me your uncle was a doctor. Now I discover he is an undertaker."

"I told you properly. Your interpretation was wrong. I said, 'He followed the medical profession.'"

****

A ninety-five-year-old hillbilly was asked how he had managed to live so long. "Easy," he replied. "When I works, I works hard and when I sits, I sits loose...and when I worries...I fall asleep."

****

"It's not good for you to be so resentful about growing old and having the disabilities of age," the doctor advised. "Just remember, many are denied the privilege."

****

"Doctor, could you explain the meaning of 'ovation' to me?"

"Well, let me put first things first," the doctor replied. "The ovulation comes first and *then* comes the ovation."

"WELL, WELL, LOOK WHAT WE HAVE HERE—C.R. PILLOBEE M.D. LET'S LEAVE HIM COOLING HIS HEELS FOR AN UNREASONABLE LENGTH OF TIME."

****

A man, poor all of his life, suddenly comes into big money. Wanting to give his daughter the very best education, he sends her to France, to school. After graduation, she returns from France, marries, becomes pregnant and is now in hospital, ready to deliver her first baby. Husband, father, mother, doctor are all in the delivery room.

"Mon dieu," the girl moans.

"Not yet," was the doctor's reply.

"Sacre bleu! Sauvez moi, Docteur," the girl moans.

"Now?" the husband inquires.

"No, not yet. Sit tight."

"Holy smokes. It hurts like hell," the girl screamed.

"Now it's time," the doctor said.

****

Dr. Pedro Gonzalos defines a reducing salon as a place that takes your breadth away.

A patient, a man terribly close with a dollar and who always complained about the size of his medical bills, got a chicken bone stuck in his throat. His wife called the doctor who hurried over and, with forceps, managed to remove the bone just prior to death! In half an hour the man was almost fully recovered and the doctor prepared to leave. "How much do I owe you for that piddly five minutes work, Doctor?"

"Just pay me half of what you'd have willingly paid me when the bone was stuck in your throat," the doctor replied.

****

An eminent Champaign, Illinois physician, Dr. Stephen Tager, told this story with such seriousness that one almost believes it is true!

It seems that Pablo Picasso spilled a bit of caustic paint in his eye and rushed to his ophthalmologist to get help. Quickly the physician did the necessary treatment and the famous painter was enormously relieved and grateful. "How much do I owe you, Doctor?" Picasso asked.

"Nothing. It is an honor to treat you, Sir," the physician replied.

"That's so generous of you...but I couldn't permit it," the painter exclaimed.

"Forget it," the doctor replied.

Back home, Picasso determined to paint a superb picture for the physician. And he did. In the upper right hand corner he painted a lovely Paris street scene. In the upper left corner, he painted a rural scene. In the lower right corner, he painted a scene of the lovely Seine River. And he placed an abstract image in the lower left corner. In the middle, he painted a large eye, wide open, lids and all. This he presented to the physician.

"Oh, thank you so much," the doctor said. "It is absolutely divine. But tell me, what is the object in the center?"

"It is an eye, Sir, honoring your noble profession."

The doctor looked quizzically at the painting, then said, "It's a damned good thing I'm not a proctologist!"

****

A medical student had delivered the baby, but the newborn child would not stop crying. The student tried everything and nothing appeased the child. Finally, the student repeated over and over, "Take it easy, Donald. Take it easy, Donald."

Soon a professor of medicine walked in, listened to the student repeat that "Take it easy, Donald."

"What's the trouble with baby Donald?" the professor asked.

"Not him, I'm Donald," the student replied.

"Not him, I'm Donald," the student replied.

The doctor was lecturing his patient on the need to reduce. "At your age, Sir, all that extra weight you carry is bound to shorten your life. Here's a drug I want you to take, and a diet regimen. I want you to take the pills and observe the diet for one month. Then I want to see three-fourths of you back here for a checkup!"

****

He took his defeat like a man...blamed it on his wife.

****

Yet another story of those obsessive patients who ain't what they seem to be:

The doctor escorted the patient to his office and had him recline on the couch. After taking his notebook and seating himself on a chair near the patient's couch, the doctor said, "Now, let's begin to talk and find out why you think you are a clock."

"No, please, Doctor. That's not my trouble! I need to find out why I chime every hour on the hour."

****

Laughter is God's hand on the shoulder of an uptight world!

****

Patient:	"I got to tell you, Doctor, that all I dream about is baseball. Nothing but that."
Psychiatrist:	"Never sex? Don't you ever dream about women?"
Patient:	"Ya think I'm nuts? If I did that I'd lose my turn at bat."

****

A man ninety years old came into his doctor's office and asked for a blood test.

"You're not thinking of getting married, are you, John?" his doctor asked.

"Yep! Sure am. That's why I need that test."

"But John...at your age...why do you want to get married?"

"Doctor, it's not that I want to, it's that I got to."

****

"Nothing I do ever seems to come out right," the patient complained to his psychiatrist. "If my ship comes into port, I'll probably be waiting at the railroad station."

****

A patient came into his doctor's office complaining of pain in his groin. "I know it's an odd place for it, Doctor, but I figure I've caught cold in my penis."

The doctor examined him, then said, "Call it a cold if you will, but until it starts sneezing, we'll treat you for V.D."

****

"I apologize for keeping you waiting for so long," the doctor told the patient as he entered the examination room.

"That's ok with me, Doctor. But it might have been better had you seen me while my ailment was in its early stages."

****

A prescription is kind of hieroglyphic that a physician writes and a druggist translates into dollar signs.

****

Nothing about the medical profession should surprise us any more. But a new hospital statement is something of a shocker. Did you know that now, after operations, they place a placard on the incision that reads: "This is a federal project showing your tax dollar is at work." (Honest).

****

"Don't be hard on yourself," Doctor Esroid told his patient. "Every man is a damn fool for at least ten minutes every day. The trick is not to exceed that limit."

****

A well-known Chicago physician said, "Modesty has ruined more kidneys than bad liquor."

****

Then there were the two hypochondriacs who had a hurt-to-hurt conversation.

The stork is a bird with a great big bill,
He brings us our babies whenever he will.
Then comes the doctor, and when he is through,
We find that he has a big bill, too.

****

Doctor Yaffee broke his glasses and had no spare. But he had a long list of patients and decided to tough it out in his office.

An old lady was the doctor's first patient and she complained of pains in her chest. So the doctor, unsure of himself, scarcely able to see her, had her disrobe, then commenced the examination of her chest. He probed about her ribs for a bit, then said, "Madam, these ribs are seriously outstanding. They protrude too far...much too far and they worry me."

The good lady replied, "Doctor Yaffee, I think you'll get a better feel of things if you'll quit messin' around with those venetian blinds of yours."

****

It seems an undebatable fact that health is the most unappreciated condition in the world...by those who have it.

****

Doctor Howard Knocks was known as the cheapest, the very tightest man on the staff. They tell the story of the time he got engaged. He announced it to his best friend, saying, "I gave her a real diamond. It was a beauty."

"Are you sure it was a genuine, real diamond, Howard?"

"It damned well better be, Buddy, or I've been screwed out of five dollars."

****

Zit Doctor:	Dermatologist.
Bug Doctor:	In prisons, the term is used to describe a psychologist or psychiatrist.
Couch Doctor:	Shrink or psychoanalyst.
Spin Doctor:	An advisor or agent, especially of a politician, who uses a partisan approach to slant a story for the media. It gets its name from the "spin" of a baseball to make it curve or slant instead of going straight.

There's often wisdom to be had from a lisp, as, e.g., "Overeating can make you thick at your stomach."

****

They were having a party at Mercy Hospital, to celebrate the fiftieth year of the institution. Each doctor and nurse was asked to create a four-line limerick. Doctor Ian Pursewatcher gave this gem:

> "There was a young lady of
> Boston, Mass.,
> Who stepped into the sea, right up to her
> ankle."

"Hey, Doc, it doesn't rhyme! It doesn't count 'cause it doesn't rhyme."
"It doesn't, eh? Just wait till the tide comes in!"

****

"I'M TAKING YOU OFF SUGAR
AND SPICE AND EVERYTHING
NICE."

A psychiatrist has labeled his very own subject, the brain. He calls it a "scheme engine!"

****

It may be only rumor, but the scuttlebutt has it that an oversexed girl was advised by her doctor to stay *out of bed for three weeks.*

****

Nat D. Dulaney, M.D. was an outstanding country doctor who practiced in and around Bristol, Tennessee, until his death in 1941. In 1939, he published a personal memoir, a kind of history of his life, thought and actions in his hometown. His publishers described him thusly: "Unselfish service and kindness were the keynotes of his life, and these together with his keen sense of humor, endeared him to all his acquaintances." Here are a few words from his book, *Speaking of Accidents.*

The descent of man means nothing -- it's the ascent that counts. When men worry about what happened in the beginning, I am reminded of the old farmer who went into the restaurant for dinner. When the waitress came around and asked him what he wanted, he said he didn't hardly know.

She says, "How about some oxtail soup?" The old man replied, "No, that's going too far back for soup."

Dr. Delaney built a home outside the town and this home had never had a name until the day the doctor fell and broke his arm. Then he gave his home the name of Dad-Gum Hill. His preacher said that, given the circumstances, "He could have made it a little stronger!"

Dr. Delaney goes on to talk about bones and tells the story of the boy who when asked to identify the spinal column replied, "It's a string of bones up your back, with your head settin' on one end and you settin' on the other."

He gives as an example of "supreme optimism" the example of "the bridegroom of seventy-five and the bride of seventy out looking for a bungalow near a public school."

The good doctor didn't much like contemporary music and the singing that accompanied it. He said, "Some people sing because they have something in their systems they have to get out, and if they can't sneeze it, they sing it."

A bum went into the doctor's office and was told, "I'll examine you thoroughly for twenty dollars." The tramp replied, "OK, Doc, and if you find it, I want half."

****

Reminiscent of *The Music Man,* is the story of the patent Medicine Man who used minstrels to entertain and beguile his audience. That flim-flam artist had medicine to cure any ailment: "My medicine is the only road that leads to health and long life," he roared.

One of his audience asked, "How about our ancestors...they didn't have your medicine." The sharpie said, "Darn right they didn't. And where are they now?"

An old-fashioned physician, the kind that relied on horse sense, once said that a doctor can find something about the condition by looking at the tongue. But more frequently, he can listen to it and get a better understanding of the case.

A country doctor went to see a patient in a one-room cabin, where he found fourteen people and three chairs. An old lady got up and said, "Doc, have this chair." The doctor replied, "No, keep your seat, I don't want to deprive you of it." The old woman answered, "You take it, Doc, there ain't no depravity in it."

The doctor was bragging that he was a self-made man. His patient looked at him and said, "Well, by golly, that sure relieves the good Lord of any awful responsibility."

At a revival, a good old brother, all crippled up with rheumatism, could hardly stand to tell the congregation what the Lord had done for him. Standing half bent, making painful gestures with his twisted fingers, he said, "Well, brethren, He's mighty near ruint me!"

****

A lawyer and a doctor were having an argument about the worth of each of their professions. "Let's say this," the doctor said, "not all lawyers are shady and reprehensible, and that's for sure. But most all agree that your job certainly doesn't make angels of men."

"I could agree on that," the lawyer replied. "In that area we don't qualify. At least not like physicians do. After all, nobody makes as many angels as the doctors."

69

Twenty-two kids had Mrs. O'Ryan.
She was fine, but the stork was dyin'.

****

Did you hear about the near-sighted physician who treated a patient for varicose veins for nearly a year before he discovered that her fountain pen leaked?

****

Sometimes the associations of physicians have a tough time deciding where to hold their conventions. For example, the gallstone surgeons searched everywhere and finally settled on the appropriate city of...Little Rock. Too, the urologists chose an appropriate place...Peoria.

****

Did you know that the medical profession has a new discipline? The trained and efficient plumbers of San Diego charge so much for their services that they now belong to the profession of...Drain Surgeons.

****

Then there was the New York psychiatrist who was convicted of gestalt with a deadly weapon.

****

It is said at the University of Illinois Medical School that orthopedists get all the breaks.

****

The doctor told the patient to try and be more upbeat, more optimistic in his life. "Just remember," the physician said, "that laughter is free, legal, has no calories, no cholesterol, no preservatives, no carcinogens and is absolutely safe. I suggest that you go to the public library, select a couple of funny books, take them home, and select five pages to be taken at bedtime."

In class at medical school, the professor was discussing *diabetes mellitus.* "It's a Greek name," he said, "with the word *mellitus* meaning 'sweet' as in honey. Now, as you know, you can often find sugar in the urine of diabetics, such as is in this flagon of urine." He held it up for all to see. "If you wonder about the sugar, it is there." Whereupon, the professor dipped one finger into the urine, then touched finger to his tongue as if tasting wine, opening and closing his lips. Then he passed the urine sample to the students, asking them to repeat his procedure and to give him their opinion. When all had completed the test, he said, "Very good...now you have learned the first principle you will need in diagnosis...the power of observation."

The students were puzzled. "You see," continued the professor, "I dipped my *middle* finger in the urine, but I licked my *index* finger, not at all like you students did it."

****

A doctor was giving an examination to a young girl. He applied the stethoscope to her chest wall and said, "Big breaths, now."

"Yeth, and I'm only thixteen," smiled the girl.

****

"You live too much in the past, Mrs. Jenkins," the psychiatrist said. "Just remember that the past is a swell place to visit but a lousy place to live in."

****

A physician who was not well liked by his colleagues, was taken ill and sent to the hospital. After a few days, he received this get-well card from his associates. "Your colleagues at the hospital have asked that we send you this card offering our best wishes for a speedy recovery. The motion was passed by ten votes to nine."

****

A doctor in an Iowa farming community was visited by a farmer who asked how much it would cost to remove an appendix.

"My usual charge is fifteen hundred dollars," said the doctor. "But in your case I'll only charge three hundred."

"How come?" said the farmer suspiciously.

"Because when you pay me, I don't lose so much money."

****

Dr. Peter Aufblau was doing some desk work in his office when in rushed a lovely young lady wearing a dress that was backless, strapless and with a skirt that came up within four inches of her....harrumph! "Doctor," she moaned, "I just feel awful. It's a cold coming on and I need help."

"Help is easily come by," said the good doctor. "Just go on home, get dressed and go to bed."

****

A doctor once put the value of a smile succinctly and wisely. "It takes 72 muscles to frown," he said, "but only 16 to smile. So if it's fatigue that bothers you, smile more."

****

If you've ever wondered about the difference between a specialist and a general practitioner, the former has his patients so well trained that they become ill only during surgery hours. But a general practitioner can be called off the golf course at any time.

****

A definition of psychiatry: The care of the id by the odd.

****

"HOW'S THE FAMILY?"

Dr. Theodore Hessinger was a very fine surgeon but, in his own mind he was far better than that...he thought himself the best in the nation and talked that way. A nurse described him in this way: "If Doctor Hessinger sat on a tack, he'd be nothing but a big hiss!"

****

Dr. Francis Leo Golden says: "Eat, drink and be merry, for tomorrow you may diet."

****

A doctor was discussing the day's patients with a friend. "I had this young girl come in for an examination. She was really thin, so thin she wore bandaids for a brassier. Wow! Was she skinny. She could have crawled through a piccolo without hitting a single note.
"And every time she yawned, her skirt fell down. Well, I x-rayed her. The only thing that showed up on the plate was the table."

****

Here's to the stork,
A most valuable bird,
That inhabits the residence districts.
He doesn't sing tunes
Nor yield any plumes,
But he helps out the vital statistics.

****

Dr. Philander Q. Doesticks used to say that when a woman has too many children, you can classify her as overbearing.

****

A surgeon, an architect and a politician were arguing about whose profession was the oldest.
"Architecture, obviously, is oldest because only an architect could have brought order out of the primordial chaos."
"Yes, but consider that a physician had to deliver Eve from Adam's rib. So that indicates a surgical job of primary proportions."
"But," said the political, "the architect is right, he came before the medical man, creating order out of chaos. But, gentlemen, who created the chaos in the first place?"

The patient was told to bathe his feet in pure sea salt water twice a day. So he went to the beach, filled two pails and started toward his car. The lifeguard, having some fun, walked to him saying, "That'll cost you two bits each pail, Sir." The man paid. A few days later, he came back to the beach at low tide, looked at the low water, then the guard, then said, "Wow! You've sure got a great business here."

****

Sometimes doctors can be truly catty. Consider the one doctor saying to the other, "I just read your new book. Interesting. Who wrote it for you?"
"I'm sure glad you enjoyed it, Doctor. But tell me, who read it to you?"

****

A wise man once said that the art of medicine consists of the ability to amuse the patient while nature cures the disease.

****

"Mrs. Peters, please be quiet and let me ask the questions and do the talking. You listen! That's the reason you have two ears and only one mouth."

****

After eating in a restaurant, old Dr. Betty Peters searched for her senior citizen's card. "That's all right, Ma'am. I don't have to see your card," said the waiter.
"Well! I thought you'd at least have the courtesy to doubt me!"

****

There once was a surgeon named Stachend,
Who limped like a soldier on rations.
Since once when a lad,
When his memory was bad,
He tried mounting a horse from the backend.

****

"The human body was designed by a wise and knowing God," the physician told his unhappy patient. "He fixed it so that you can't pat yourself on the back nor kick your own backside."

There was a meeting for patients and relatives of those who had undergone open-heart surgery. The doctor explained something about the procedures involved, arterial grafts, heart valves and the like, then said, "You know, folks, doctors are really glorified plumbers." A voice was heard from the audience. "Good gosh, Doc, your fees ain't gonna be that high, are they?"

****

Doctor Frederick Peters was making a call through unfamiliar farm country. He stopped to ask for directions to the farm home requiring his service. "Am I on the road to Gerald Corrigan's farm?" he asked?

"Yep!"

"And how far is it from here?"

"Well, I tell ya...if ya keep on the direction you are headin', it's twenty five thousand miles. If you turn around and go back on this road, it's about six!"

****

Tall tales are favorites of all Americans, not least the physicians. Here a couple of doozies:

The son of a Texas physician boasted to his college buddy that his father owned and operated his own plane.

"That's not so unusual," the friend replied. "Lots of my friends own and fly a plane."

"In the house?" was the Texan's retort.

****

Then there is the tale of the Texas physician who had a car full of little kids clamoring for ice cream cones. So he stopped the car in front of an ice cream store, went inside and ordered thirty ice cream cones. "I need 'em for the thirty kids I got in the car outside!"

"Thirty kids? Wow! what nationality are they?" the clerk asked.

"They're Texans," replied the physician.

"You're kidding," exclaimed the clerk. "Texans are all big guys! Six foot and tall. Real tall, not like those little kids."

"They were tall," replied the physician. "But they'd been eating too many Texas beans and felt bad. So I gave them all enemas and, as you can see, that reduced 'em to proper size."

****

One of the healthiest things a man can have up his sleeve is...a funny bone.

Dr. Charles Egan, M.D., was a fine physician with only one fault. He hated to spend money. Take it in? Yes. Spend it? No. Well, one day, he staggered into his office almost out of breath, gasping and heaving. Exhausted.

"What happened, Dr. Egan?" his nurse said, taking him by the arm.

"The bus...the bus..."

"The bus caused this? But how could it?"

"I was...not riding...was running behind...the... bus."

"Oh. To save money?"

"Yes."

"But it really isn't so far from your home to this office."

"I know, but the bus...was going...the other way."

****

" `...AND ALL THE KING'S HORSES AND ALL THE KING'S MEN COULDN'T PUT HUMPTY DUMPTY TOGETHER AGAIN.' —SO HE SUED THE WHOLE BUNCH OF 'EM FOR PRACTICING MEDICINE WITHOUT A LICENSE !"

You can always tell an optimistic physician from a pessimistic one. The former goes to the window every morning and says, "Good morning, Lord." The pessimist goes to the window and says, "Good Lord, morning."

****

An intern was examining his first case and he was terribly nervous over it. He followed instructions to the letter in conducting the examination: weight, height, blood count and blood pressure, and so on. He applied the thermometer for a temperature reading, following which he asked the patient to sit down and answer questions on the examination form. "Please, Sir, sit down for some questions," he said.

The patient replied, "Doctor, wouldn't it be better if you took the thermometer out of my bottom first?"

****

Then there's the story of the famous blues singer who went to her doctor complaining of chest pains. The doctor examined her carefully with a stethoscope, moving the sound inlet from place to place over the body, trying one place after another.

"Hey, good Doctor," she said. "Can't you find a program that suits you?"

****

Many Americans have the "right stuff," but too many of those who have it have it in the wrong place.

****

Perhaps it is professional jealousy, but a medical internist once described a psychiatrist as "a medical doctor who's compassionate for the cashinit!"

****

"Sure I smoke," the patient told his physician. "Two packs a day and have for thirty years."

"Really? Two packs a day?"

"You betcha. And I also puff on cigars and pipes..."

"And stairs?" the doctor added.

"Mr. Jones," the physician counseled, "I want you to relax more, take life easier. I suggest that you get a job with the government."

****

A lawyer and a doctor were chatting together at the club, both complaining about clients and patients who asked for advice when away from the office...free advice. "I put an end to that," the doctor boasted. "What do you do?" asked the lawyer.

"Well, when they start telling me about what ails them, I immediately ask them to disrobe. And that seems to end the matter."

****

"Try to have your bowel movement, as well your worrying, done before breakfast," the psychiatrist advised.

****

Then there was the physician who advised all couples intending marriage to use condoms on all conceivable occasions.

****

"Young man," Doctor Cynthia Brown cautioned her patient, "I'm telling you this for your own good. I don't want you to follow in your parents' fatsteps."

****

An award was given to Dr. Hugo Hagandis for discovering a true definition for a neurotic: "A person afflicted with perpetual emotion."

****

The doctor examined the patient for ulcers, then advised him to quit worrying so much: "Most ulcers are caused by mountain climbing over molehills."

****

Doctors seem to cherish puns, at least sometimes: Here are a few: "I'm at your cervix," said the gynecologist. "I just can't be 'Jung' forever," said the psychiatrist. Then there was the acupuncturist who remarked, "I've reached the 'point' of no return."

DEPRECIATION

Come income tax time, a doctor
    Must rally his faltering senses
And gather his files all about him
    And search through his stubs for expenses.

Then, worn from the calls he's been making
    At three and at four in the morning,
And patients with ailments that baffle
    And births without adequate warning,

He thinks, as he peers at the mirror
    That faces him over the shelf,
That they ought to allow a deduction
    For wear and tear on himself.

(*The Medical Muse* by Richard Armour, 1963. McGraw-Hill Book Co., New York, NY. Reprinted with permission of Mrs. Kathleen S. Armour, Claremont, CA)

****

A woman sees her doctor and tells him that she realizes she's older each day, but that her lack of interest in sex is in sharp contrast to her husband's needs. She is terribly worried about it. Can the doctor help her?

"I think so," the doctor said. "There is a new pill out. Here are four of them. Now you take only one-half a pill each day and see how things work. Come see me in ten days."

But in just three days the woman is back. "Doctor, what kind of pills were those? They've about ruined my marriage. Last night, it was terrible. It was awful. I know you told me to take one-half a pill but I took all four of them."

"My goodness. And what happened?"

"Well, in the middle of our dinner, I had this overwhelming impulse not only to make love to my hubby but to...well...to rape him. I jumped up and pulled him on top of the table...I can hardly speak of it...knocked over two water glasses, broke several dishes and the tablecloth is a mess. Shameful behavior."

"This is terrible. You're right. And even though you didn't follow instructions, I feel partly responsible, those broken dishes and all. At least let me pay to replace them."

"Forget it, Doctor. It's for sure they're never gonna let us in that restaurant again."

****

Psychiatrist: "Tell me, Sir...when did you first discover that you enjoyed paying income tax?"

"Doc," said the old Tennessee farmer, leading a gangling young man up to the physician. "Help my son-in-law out, willya? I shot him in the laig, yisterday and he needs fixin' up."

"Shame! For shame!" the doctor exclaimed. "Shooting your very own son-in-law!"

"Waal, Doc," the farmer said. "Yesterday when ah shot him...he weren't mah son-in-law!"

****

"Your trouble," the doctor advised his elderly patient, "is that you are a senior citizen trying to keep up with the freshman class."

****

They tell the story at medical meetings of a patient who steadfastly refused to pay his medical bills. Finally, he bought a book on medicine and, with the help of the book, he treated himself successfully for many years. But, eventually, he died of a misprint.

****

A young lady, just beginning the pangs of puberty, came into the doctor's office to tell him some of her physical problems. After she had explained, the doctor asked her if she knew the first and best oral contraceptive.

"No!" she replied.

"That's right!" said the doctor.

****

"Doctor, I had one helluva time with that prescription you gave me."

"Why it was simple enough. I told you to take two aspirins at bedtime and follow that with a hot bath."

"Yeah, I know. Trouble wasn't with the aspirins, Doc. But I couldn't get but about 10 percent of that hot bath down me. As it is, my stomach goes in and out with the tide."

****

Where are you going, my pretty maid?
I'm going to cut the corn, she said.
Can I go with you, my pretty maid?
If you're a chiropodist, yes, she said.

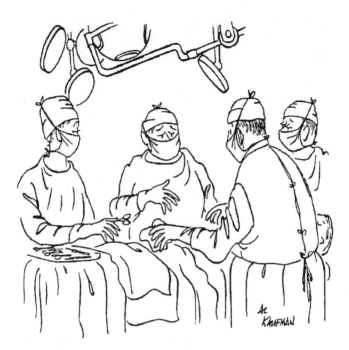

"You have to WHAT?"
(Reprinted with permission of *Medical Economics)*

****

It seems that good jokes never die, they just take on new forms. Here are a few from fifty-five years ago from *The Master Book of Humorous Quotations,* by Leewin B. Williams (Abingdon-Cokesbury Press, Nashville).
"I say, Doctor, did you ever doctor another doctor?"
"Oh yes, often."
"Well, tell me this: does a doctor doctor a doctor the way the doctored doctor wants to be doctored, or does the doctor doing the doctoring doctor the other doctor in his own way?"

****

Why is it that when a woman tells a doctor she's completely tuckered out, he immediately looks at her tongue?

****

A hillbilly describes his diarrhea to his doctor: "I've got the whistlebelly thumps and the backdoor trots."

Once an old man visited a doctor and was given definite instructions as to what he should do. Shaking his head, he started to leave the office, when the doctor said, "Hey! One minute. You forgot to pay me."

"Pay you? For what?"

"For my medical advice?"

"Heck no! I ain't agonna take it!"

****

Medical students at Rush Medical College had an unusual way of remembering parts of the anatomy. They named the body parts after people and things and then put them in a sequence that helped them recall the actual names. An example: Asked to name the wrist bones, they would recite to themselves this ditty, "Never lower Tillie's pants, Mother might come home." This helped them recall the follow parts: navicular, lunate, triangle, pisiform, greater multangular, lesser multangular, capitate, hamate.

****

A possible theme song for doctors concerned with the genito-urinary tract: "To Pee the Impossible Stream."

****

In bygone days, before women had the right to vote, a physician found himself in a hot argument with a woman patient. She argued on and on about the equality of women and the shame in their being denied the right to vote. At last she said, "So tell me, Doctor...What's the difference, the distinction, between a man and a woman?"

The doctor thought for a moment, then replied, "I can't conceive!"

****

Doctor, after a long, hard day, "I feel powerful tired, just like I got one wheel down and my axle draggin'."

****

An ignorant old lady from the hills of Arkansas visited a physician in Little Rock. "Tell me, Madam," the doctor said, "Are you aware of Medicare?"

"Ah sho am, Doc. Ah took it for nigh onto a month and lost ten pounds."

One of the physicians at a popular health resort was looking over his books one day, comparing his list of patients. "I had a great many more patients last year than I have in this," he remarked to his wife. "I wonder where they have all gone?"

"Well, never mind, dear," she replied. "All we can do is hope for the best."

****

Physicians can't do much to help a man who sows wild oats six days a week except to counsel him to go to church on Sundays and pray for a crop failure.

****

A man by the name of Williams died and went to Heaven. When he arrived at the pearly gates, he said to St. Peter, "Well, I'm here."

"What's your name?" asked St. Peter.

"John Williams," was the reply.

St. Peter looked through the book and shook his head. "You don't belong here," he said.

"But I'm sure I belong here," said the man.

"Wait a minute," said St. Peter. He looked again, and on the last page of the book he found the name.

"Sure," said St. Peter, "you belong here, but you weren't expected for twenty years. Who's your doctor?"

****

"Doctor," an elderly gentleman now ninety years old, said, "If I'd known that I would live this long, I'd have taken a lot better care of myself."

****

Three fathers paced the floor in the obstetrics waiting room. A nurse rushed in and said to one man, "Sir, you are the father of twins."

"Hey, that's great. Especially so since I'm a member of the Minnesota Twins ball team."

Soon the nurse came back and announced to the second fellow that he was the father of triplets.

"Wonderful!" exclaimed papa number two. "What a coincidence because I'm with the 3-M Company."

The third expectant father sprang to his feet, grabbed his coat and started out. "Man, I ain't staying around here. I work for 7-Up."

Years ago and late one stormy night, a physician was aroused from sleep by a loud knocking on his door. It was a farmer who lived several miles out in the country. The farmer, who had a reputation of being "a little near," first inquired how much the doctor charged for country calls.

"Three dollars," snapped the doctor, impatient that the fellow would bargain under such circumstances.

Thereupon the farmer urged him to drive to his home immediately. So the doctor dressed and the two of them drove to the farmer's house with as much speed as the muddy, slippery roads permitted. As soon as they arrived, the farmer stepped out of the auto, took three dollars from his pocket and handed them to the doctor.

"But where is my patient?" demanded the physician.

"There ain't none," answered the country man, "but that taxi driver would have charged me five dollars to bring me out here tonight."

****

In the straw: A country phrase to describe a woman in labor or giving birth, pregnant. The phrase is thought to have originated because the mattresses used during childbirth were filled with straw. Also, straw was placed on the wooden entrance stairs of the house, where the woman was giving birth, to dull the sound and eliminate fright.

****

Mother: "My daughter has me worried, running around with that new doctor in town."
Friend: "Not to worry! Just feed her an apple a day."

****

Medical authorities tell us that it is not, repeat not, the fall that causes most injuries, it is the sudden stop.

****

Husband: "Well, Mabel, I did as you wanted me to do...I saw the doctor today about my memory loss and the trouble I have remembering things."
Wife: "Well, tell me, what did he say you should do?"
Husband: "What I should do? He said I should pay him in advance."

Patient: "Doctor, I'm fifty now. Do you think I'll live to be eighty?"
Doctor: "Well, do you drink, smoke, chase women, or gamble?"
Patient: "I don't drink. I never smoked. I rarely gamble and I never run around with women."
Doctor: "Then tell me...why in hell do you want to live to be eighty?"

****

Veterinarians are now prescribing birth control pills for dogs. They call it an anti-litter campaign.

****

(*Never Try To Teach A Pig To Sing*. Reprinted with permission of Wayne State University Press).

****

Doctor: "How can I help you, Madam?"
Woman: "I don't need help, Doctor, it's my husband. He never quits worrying about money, day and night he frets and tosses and suffers, worrying about money."
Doctor: "I can relieve him of that!"

On the blink: Unwell, out of condition, not in working order. It comes from a farm term for milk gone sour, or "blinky."

****

The young parents were having trouble coping with their first child, who was a little dickens. The pediatrician reassured them with this analysis: "Science now knows that insanity is hereditary...parents generally get it from their children."

****

Physicians may be surprised and gratified to learn of several New England cures for this, that and t'other thing, back in 1896, as prescribed by Clifton Johnson in his book, *What They Say in New England.*

When you have rheumatism, carry a potato in your pocket. The potato will become hard after a time, and believers in its virtues affirm that this is because of the rheumatism it has absorbed. Also, if you carry a horse chestnut (buckeye) in your pocket, you will not be troubled by rheumatism.

If your eyes are weak, have your ears bored just as you would for earrings. That will make your eyes strong.

Testimony: "I had a great-aunt that used to have the cramps terrible till someone told her to tie a cotton string around her ankle. After that, she never had a cramp to the end of her days."

Nightmares and their cure: When you go to bed, you just smell your stockings after you've taken them off. That's all you've got to do. Warranted that you won't have any more nightmares.

A sure cure for baldness: Wash your head with sage tea and it will make a new growth of hair.

If you have a sore throat, tie one of the stockings you have worn through the day around your neck when you go to bed. The sore throat can't stand that, and will have left by morning. Be sure to tie the stocking with the hollow of the foot next to the throat.

Put the first aching tooth you have pulled in a glass of whiskey. Then drink the whiskey, and you won't ever have another tooth pulled because of toothache.

****

The more waist the less speed.

****

A person without a sense of humor is like an auto without shocks...jolted by every bump in the road.

There was a young medic from Wheeling,
Blessed with such delicate feeling,
When he read, on the door,
"Don't spit on the floor,"
He leaped up and spat on the ceiling.

****

Dr. Brown borrowed a pen from Dr. Edgars, then returned it, whereupon Dr. Edgars said furiously, "You broke my pen! It's useless. What are you going to do about it?"

Whereupon Dr. Brown replied, "You're crazy, man. I never borrowed your pen. And secondly, it was in first-rate condition when I handed it to you. What's more, it was broken when you loaned it to me."

****

Dr. Ivan Burns lived in Arizona and had a great medical practice, a fine family of two sons and two daughters, all married. But his one disappointment in life was that none of his kids had given him grandchildren. Not one. So, at Thanksgiving dinner at his home, with sons and daughters and their spouses all gathered around the festive table, he announced as follows: "I keep hoping that one or all of you will bless me with grandchildren but, so far, I have none. But I still hope. Yesterday, I went to the bank and set up a trust fund of five hundred thousand dollars to be given to my first grandchild. But now, before we eat, let us say grace. Please bow your heads."

And do you know that when the prayer was done and the good doctor looked up, he and his wife were the only ones remaining at the table.

****

They say there is a doctor in Joliet, Illinois, who is always ready to lend a helping hand to anyone having trouble opening his pocketbook.

****

The psychiatrist had a wonderful bit of advice that she gave to patients distraught over money worries. "Always learn to live within your means," she would tell them, "even if you have to borrow money to do it."

The elderly physician gave this bit of advice to her younger, physically exhausted assistant: "The reason you feel dog-tired is because you did nothing but growl all day."

****

A family physician advised the young couple, vastly troubled by the unmanageable child as follows:

"My suggestion to you is to follow the advice of this advertisement that appeared in the local newspaper."

GUARANTEED TO AMUSE ANY CHILD. ABSOLUTELY SAFE. NO NEED TO WIND. NO BATTERIES REQUIRED. PORTABLE. CAN ADJUST TO ANY AREA. FOR DETAILED INFORMATION, DIAL: 1-800-GRANDPARENTS

****

The man told the physician, "Doctor, I feel so lethargic, so listless and without pep. Nothing seems to excite me. Can you give me something?"

"Sir, you'll find all you need when you get my bill."

****

A patient complained of the age of some of the doctor's magazines out in his waiting room. "If you think I have old magazines," the doctor replied, "you should see the dates on a few of my patients' unpaid medical bills."

****

There was a rich doc of Nantucket,
Who kept all his cash in a bucket.
> But his daughter named Nan,
> Ran away with a man,
Now about that bucket, Nantucket.

****

A DOCTOR'S ADVICE
No matter how frigid you're feeling,
A smile adds quickness to healing.
> It grows in a wreath,
> All around the front teeth,
Thus preserving the face from congealing.
Anthony Euwer

For a bit of diversion to lighten the stress of her intense medical practice, a physician used to play the daily lottery offered by the State of Illinois. She had played the lottery since its inception. Finally, she won...a $3,000,000 prize. And she was overwhelmed. When she'd recovered sufficiently, she hurriedly called her husband and blurted, "Sir, how would you like to be made violent love to by a doctor who has just come into several million bucks."

The husband hesitated, stuttered, hemmed and haw'd a bit, then said, "Gosh, you do pose a difficult...I...really...I...well, is she good-looking?"

****

****

A sad doctor from far Alabama,
Always spoke with a bothersome stammer.
    The b-bane of my life
    Is m-m-my wife
D-d-d-d-d-d-d-dammer!

Then there was the irritable pediatrician who was everywhere known to have little patients.

****

Did you hear about the medical student who was called to the dean's office. Terribly worried, the young student walked into the office and stood before the dean's desk. "Academically, you are doing just fine," the Dean said. "But you've got to learn how to write a little less clearly."

****

Question: "How many doctors does it take to screw in a light bulb?"
Answer: "The solution depends on whether or not the light bulb has health insurance."

****

Dr. Folsom was a crotchety old cuss who didn't much like contemporary customs. Of modern female dress, he remarked that it was much like barbed wire...protects the property without obstructing the view. He also developed, created, composed the following observation about modern bathing suits:
>Mary had a bathing suit,
> The latest style, no doubt;
>And when she got inside it, she,
> Was more than half-way out.

****

It's amazing how truth can sometimes be revealed by typographical errors, as here:
"The doctor felt the patient's purse and confirmed that there was nothing he could do."

****

An American college student took a trip to England where he happened to meet a high-born lady. He spoke disparagingly of the British system of peerage, royalty and all such non-American customs. The lady was upset and said, "Sir, I'll have you know that my father is an English peer."
"Well, whatdya know," the kid replied. "Your dad is an English peer and mine is an American doc. We'll get along just fine."

90

A friend walked into the drugstore to find the owner and pharmacist hopping around and laughing like crazy. "What's going on here?" he asked.

"Well, it's plumb wonderful. Things really even out, don't they?" the druggist chortled.

"Maybe. But just what do you mean?" asked the friend.

"Well, you recall that day last winter when we came in to find our pipes all frozen?"

"Yep, sure was cold that day."

"Well, the plumber I called to fix them just came in to have a prescription filled."

****

HIPPOCRATES AND THE LATER GREEKS
by Richard Armour

Hippocrates

Before Hippocrates, medicine was in the hands of priests. (In other words, D.D.'s, not M.D.'s). The priests thought diseases were caused by demons and angry gods, which still sounds pretty plausible. But Hippocrates thought sickness could be traced to natural causes, such as bad diet, lack of fresh air, too much carousing around, and falling off the top of the Parthenon.

"In truth we know little or nothing of Hippocrates," says one historian, preparatory to writing of him at length. It seems Hippocrates was born in 460 B.C. and lived until about 355 B.C., which, if our subtraction is correct, made him 105 years old at the time of his death. His ability to keep himself alive so long must have been one reason he gained the confidence of his patients.

But if Hippocrates lived a long time, think of the large plane tree, still pointed out as the one under whose shade he once taught his pupils. The age of this tree is estimated at around 2,500 years, which shows that it knows a few things about health unknown to Hippocrates. But then, it stays out in the fresh air more than Hippocrates did, though it gets less exercise.

Hippocrates was born on the island of Cos, which explains the title of one of his many treatises, *The Cos and Effect of Disease*. Legend has it that he was once a librarian and was forced to flee when he burned some old medical books. Why he burned these books is not known. Did they disagree with his theories? An overworked librarian, was he tired of putting them back on the right shelf when they were misplaced by careless medical students? Was he cold, and out of kindling? The reader is left to his own conjectures.

Whether or not Hippocrates was forced to flee because of something he did as a librarian, there seems no doubt that he was an itinerant doctor. Since he had no office and for some reason declined to make house calls, he had to treat patients wherever he found them--on the streets (accident victims), in the groves of Academe, or in the public bath. The bath was perhaps the most convenient, because patients wishing a thorough examination were already disrobed and ready to go. Anyhow, Hippocrates kept on the move, looking for a good plague. As Hippocrates' reputation grew, people came to him from all over Greece. This was flattering to Hippocrates but not to the patient's own doctor.

"What's this Hippocrates got that I haven't got?" the family physician would ask, with just a trace of a sneer. But there was no reply, because his former patients were too busy packing to go look for Hippocrates. There was a report he was last seen in Macedonia. Or was it Thrace? With Hippocrates wandering around looking for patients and patients wandering around looking for Hippocrates, there was a good deal of confusion.

Hippocrates based his medical practice on observation and reasoning, which have been the foundation of medicine ever since. For example he would ask a patient to stick out his tongue, and he would look at it (observation). If it had a layer of whitish stuff on it, he would say to himself, "Aha, he had vanilla ice cream for dessert!" (reasoning). He was less interested in treatment than in diagnosis. Once he had figured out what was the matter with a patient and had told him, he felt he had discharged his responsibility. From then on, the patient could do the worrying. He was the one who was sick, wasn't he? (Hippocrates believed it was up to nature to do the healing. He referred his patients to nature the way GP's today refer their patients to specialists.)

Itinerant doctor

An example of Hippocrates' method of practice was the time the King of Macedonia fell sick and his doctors thought he had phthisis. (If you have trouble pronouncing "phthisis," you might be interested to know that one of Hippocrates' biographers was named Tzetzes.) Hippocrates was called in for a consultation and recognized at once that the King didn't have phthisis--he was off his rocker. Did Hippocrates attempt to cure the King? Did he tell the King, "Sire, you are nuts"? No, Hippocrates, who not only knew how to diagnose but when to keep his mouth shut, headed back to Athens as fast as he could go. Hippocrates has been called the Ideal Physician, and no wonder.

There are some fascinating legends about Hippocrates. One is that he never gave a thought to money. Another is that he admitted his errors. The reader should keep in mind that these are legends.

Ever since Hippocrates, graduating medical students take the Hippocratic oath, which starts out, "I swear." After they have been in practice a few years they learn how right Hippocrates was, and how much there is to swear about.

(*The Medical Muse* by Richard Armour, 1963. McGraw-Hill Book Co., New York, NY. Reprinted with permission of Mrs. Kathleen S. Armour, Claremont, CA)

Vance Randolph was an indefatigable collector of Arkansas folk tales. In his book, *We Always Lie To Strangers* (Columbia University Press, 1951), he told this fetching story about the difference in handling the remains of doctors between the Ozarks and at least one big city.

HOW TO GET RID OF DOCTORS

ONE TIME there was a city man come to a little settlement, and he seen a lot of people milling around in the graveyard. So he asked the folks, "What is going on over there?" A country fellow says that Doc Pendergast is dead, and we are giving him a big funeral. Doc was a prominent citizen and well fixed, also he was the best doctor in the whole country.

"Hell," says the city man, "do you bury doctors here?" The country fellow says of course they do, because when a doctor dies he has got to be buried the same as anybody else. The city man just shook his head, like he never heard of such a thing. "They sure have got some peculiar customs in Arkansas," says he.

The country fellow didn't return no answer, but he kept thinking about it. Next day he seen the city man setting on the porch of the hotel. "Mister," says he, "when a doctor dies back where you come from, what do they do with the body?" The city man says the folks just lay him out in his office and lock the door, but leave the window open. When they unlock the door next morning the doctor is gone, and that's all there is to it. The country fellow was mighty surprised to hear about such a thing. "But what becomes of the corpse?" asks he.

The city man looked kind of uneasy. "Nobody knows exactly," he says, "and we don't never talk about it, out of respect for the kinfolks. But there ain't no denying," says he, "that a doctor's office always smells like brimstone in the morning."

Here's another Vance Randolph folk tale from the hills of Arkansas. He presented it in his collection, *Hot Springs and Hell*.

DOC HOLTON OUGHT TO KNOW

Our carpenter was making a coffin out in front of his shop, and he told one of the loafers it was for old Deacon Buxton. "Hell," says the fellow, "old Buxton ain't dead!" The carpenter just went on a-driving his nails. "Doc Holton told me to make a coffin for Deacon Buxton," says he. "I reckon Doc knows what he *give* him."

2

HOSPITALS

An Iowa City, Iowa, dermatologist loved to tell tall tales. "I was passing the Animal Hospital on Twelfth Street," he said, "and they were treating a near-sighted porcupine."

"What happened that would put a porcupine in the animal hospital?" a colleague asked.

"The poor thing mistook a cactus plant for his mate."

****

It's fun to look at typographical newsprint errors. But this one took the cake. "Born to Mr. and Mrs. Jonas Haw at Memorial Hospital, a sin."

****

A grandmother, afflicted with old-age diabetes, could not stay on her rigid diet. She constantly cheated. Finally, they admitted her to the hospital where, due to overcrowding, they put the old girl in the maternity ward where, one day, her little granddaughter came to visit her. During the doctor's rounds, the little girl was asked to step outside the door. A visitor saw her and asked, "Little girl, what are you doing in the maternity ward? Are you sure you should be here?"

"I'm visiting my grandma," was her reply.

"Grandmother! What on earth is she doing on the maternity ward?"

"Oh," the little girl replied, "She's been cheating again!"

****

It seems that Patrick Michael O'Brien refused to have the operation the doctors had scheduled.

"Why are you delaying, Mr. O'Brien?" the nurse asked. "You do need it, you know."

"Maybe I do but not by the doc they assigned me."

The nurse looked at the chart and read, "Doctor Edward Kilpatrick!"

****

So the manager hands me this job...and it's about as tough to do as puttin' socks on a rooster.

A happy father, just told that he was the parent of triplets, rushed to the hospital and up to the maternity ward where he precipitately entered his wife's room. A nurse rushed up to him and led him outside. "You can't come in here from the street," she said, "with your germ-ridden clothes and dirty hands. Sir, you are not sterile!"

"Sis, you sure got that right," the new father said, grinning broadly.

****

Mary walked into her second-grade classroom and solemnly told the teacher that her brother had been taken to the hospital. "They took out his utensils," she said.

****

The tradition of the Scotch being penurious and penny-pinching endures. Recently they told the story of a woman in the hospital who needed blood transfusions. A young Scotsman volunteered. The woman gladly gave him one hundred dollars. She cut back to fifty dollars for the second pint. But she only thanked him for the third pint. It seems that she had so much Scotch blood in her by that time that a thanks was all she could muster.

****

"It's not the ups and downs and jiggles of hospital life that bothers me," said the business manager of the hospital, "It's the jerks."

****

Edgar had been a hospital employee for many years and was known for his stubborn nature. When the hospital developed a pension plan, Edgar refused to sign. This was quite serious because the arrangement depended on 100 percent cooperation and participation of employees. Everyone pleaded, argued, cajoled and in every way tried to get Edgar to go along with the entire staff, to no avail.

Finally, the janitor, a huge guy, came up to him and said, "Edgar, you bastard, if you don't sign this agreement...and right now...I'll break every bone in your g... d.... body." Well it turns out, Edgar took his pen and signed.

"So tell me," demanded the janitor, "How come it took you so damned long to sign?"

"You're the first one who's properly explained it to me!"

There was a class for new employees of the Lincoln Memorial Hospital, and the director was explaining things. "Just remember this, Folks, when you begin to feel like complaining. It's true that the squeaking wheel gets the grease, but, even more significant is the fact that the quacking duck gets shot."

****

Here are some useful definitions circulated around a Minneapolis hospital in 1932:

Bacteria:	The back door of...what else...a cafeteria.
Nourishing food:	The milk of human kindness.
Osteopathy:	A lazy man's gymnastics.
Phrenology:	The science of picking the pocket through the scalp. (Ambrose Bierce).
Skeleton:	What is left of a human when you take their insides out and their outsides off.
Spinal Column:	A thing where your head sits on one end and you sit on the other.
Stork:	A bird with a big bill.
Worry:	Interest we pay on trouble before it is due.

****

*"Why, no--I thought **you** would close."*
(Reprinted with permission of *Medical Economics*)

There's a sign at the entrance to the Los Angeles General Hospital that reads, "WHAT SUNSHINE IS TO FLOWERS, SMILES ARE TO HUMAN BEINGS."

****

I don't know how she holds her job in the admissions office. Why, every time her typewriter bell rings, she thinks it's time for a coffee break.

****

One day a young girl approached the desk in the maternity ward. She was, as the boys say, "carrying the bass drum." As was normal procedure, the nurse on duty questioned her and filled in the answers on a questionnaire. She needed to know names, doctors and all the rest. But the girl did not recall the father's name for the medical history.

"Do you know anything about him at all?" the nurse asked incredulously.

"Not really," the poor mother-to-be replied.

"Not even the color of his hair, maybe?" asked the nurse.

"The sucker never took his hat off," was the reply.

****

His wife's mother was in desperate need of a blood transfusion. But she had such an unusual type of blood that the hospital attendants could not find a proper donor for her. "Oh, it's awful," moaned the daughter of the old lady. She turned to her husband. "Dear, what can we do?"

"Suggest that they try, they try, a...a...tiger!" was his suggestion.

****

"I'd purely love to take over thiseyer job amangin' thiseyer hospital," said the second assistant manager. "I'd shore change thangs around chere."

"Forget it," said his buddy. "You got about as much chance of gettin' that job as a grasshopper has in a henhouse."

****

Mary had a little lamb,
The lamb had halitosis.
So at the hospital where Mary worked,
The people held their nosis.

A hospital is a place where, when you finally get to sleep, they awaken you to give you a sleeping pill.

****

"Don't try to put me at ease about it, Doctor," the intern said to the instructing physician. "Just tell me if you think I got the stuff it takes to be a doctor. Take the bull by the tail, Sir, and look the matter square in the face."

****

Perhaps this sign should be posted in a conspicuous place in all hospitals: "WARNING: HUMOR MAY BE HAZARDOUS TO YOUR ILLNESS."

****

She was a pretty little redhead
     Sitting there upon the bed,
Looking very cute and shy
     At every doctor passing by.
Such lovely eyes,
     ecstatic thighs --
It's too bad
     She's bald!

****

First man: "I knew that Pete Kurlitis'd never make it through medical school."
Second man: "What do you mean? I always thought Pete was reasonably smart."
First man: "Pete smart? You must be kiddin'. Why if brains were leather, Pete Kurlitis wouldn't have enough to saddle a flea."

****

It is a rather old story but too good to let die. It goes like this. A patient in the hospital had bad gastric ulcers so that it was necessary to feed him with a rectal tube. His nurse, a cute blonde, had been faithfully attentive to him and the patient was grateful. One day, after a rectal breakfast, the patient held the nurse's arm and said, "You've been truly kind and attentive to me, Nurse, and I'm grateful. I have an idea. Why don't you get another tube and have lunch with me?"

The last joke reminds us that old jokes never die...they just smell that way.

****

Herman and Clara had lived all their lives far back in the mountains and neither had had much schooling. They'd planned to have their baby in the cabin but the old doctor thought otherwise. So they took Clara to a Little Rock hospital where Herman came to visit her.

"Herman, you ain't gonna b'lieve this," Clara told him, smiling broadly.

"Believe what, Honey?" Herman asked.

"I just couldn't believe my eyes," said Clara. "They got them faucets in thiseyer bathroom initialed especially fer us. Ain't that dandy?"

****

It's hotter in here than honeymoon sheets.

****

"I see by your chart that you've had some complications..."

****

A farmer was served his first meal in the hospital. It was a ham sandwich. He looked between the two slices, at the ham in between, then turned to the nurse and said, "Nurse, your cook damned near missed when cuttin' this ham."

100

The nurses detested a certain doctor. One of them said of him,"It's true that the jerk was bred in Alabama, but he's only a crumb around here."

****

Hospitals are getting almost too large. It seems that you determine that it really is too large when it takes five or six days for gossip to get from one end of the building to the other.

****

The obstetrics nurse was getting a bit bored with babies, babies, babies. Finally, she described the cute little things as an alimentary canal with a loud voice at one end and complete irresponsibility at the other.

****

In Peoria, Illinois, they tell the story of a farmer who had an attack of appendicitis. They put him in the hospital, operated and removed the appendix. The next morning the surgeon met the guy in the hall, **fully dressed** and ready to check out. "Sir!" the physician exploded. "You can't leave this hospital so soon! And it is dangerous for you to be walking around like this. You could bust your stitches."

"What the hell are you tellin' me, Doc? You mean to say you been using cheap thread?"

****

When they brought him to emergency, he was mashed flatter than a fritter.

****

The nurse brought the new baby out of delivery and showed him the lovely child. "Sir, he looks just like you," she said, beaming.

"Nice of you to say so. But let me tell you of a new poem that came to me while you walked out here."

You say the baby looks like me?
How sad, I surely dread it.
But the only likeness I can see,
Is that we're both bald-headed.

The heating system in a country hospital malfunctioned so that the place was inordinately hot. One of the country patients described the examination room as "hotter than a June bride's featherbed."

****

Mary Petefish is in Memorial Hospital after a severe fall from a horse. She has recovered sufficiently so that she can see her friends.

****

A New York hospital administrator was discovered perverting the accounts payable so that he managed to steal a good deal of money from his hospital. He was described by one of his fellow workers as so crooked he could hide behind a corkscrew. Others described him as so crooked that he had to screw his pants off.

****

Americans have a savvy way of putting things. Consider this description of a man who got an administrative job at the hospital-- to the great surprise of folks who knew him. They described the event in this way:

"It's good to know that Eddie got that hospital job. But it worries me. I happen to know that Eddie couldn't track an elephant in three feet of snow! His head is empty as last year's bird's nest."

****

A wise and experienced nurse once remarked to a patient, who complained bitterly about his constant coughing, "Just remember this, Sir. It's not the cough that carries you off, it's the coffin they carry you offin."

****

The patient called the nurse into his room. "Nurse, could you give me the phone number of a florist? I want to order flowers and give them to your telephone operator."

"I'll be glad to get a number for you. And I want to thank you for thinking of it. She'll be so happy to get them."

"Happy? To get them?" the patient replied. "But I thought she was dead!"

102

During World War II, a cute trick was played on a much disliked Sergeant Major in the Infantry. One of the men in his unit decided to get even with him, so he put on an orderly's white uniform, then went to the Sergeant Major's hospital room and told him to turn over in bed, to rest on his stomach, that it was time for a rectal thermometer. The Sergeant turned over and the GI placed the object in his rectum, then excused himself as he said he must leave for an urgent assignment.

Nearly an hour passed and the Sergeant was really upset at having to contain that thermometer in his rectum all that time. Finally a nurse showed up. She stopped at the bedside and said, "What's going on here, Sergeant?"

"Why, they're taking my temperature. But why so long, I don't know."

"Taking your temperature, Sergeant?"

"That's right, dammit. Can't you see!"

"I can see, all right. But with a *daffodil?*"

****

When in the hospital, guard your rear. Don't forget it's enema country.

****

In Chicago, a phone call was received at the hospital. "Do you have John Sexauer as a patient?"

"A what?" the operator asked.

"Sexauer. That's it...Sexauer."

"Mister, we don't even get a coffee break in this place."

****

Fatigue is a chronic condition among physicians, nurses and staff at many hospitals of the nation. Here are some telling phrases used to describe all-too-common fatigue:

I feel and look like a bar of soap after Saturday night's bath.

Man, I'm beginning to feel like I was born tired and suffered a relapse.

I got up so early this morning, I had to pry up the sun with a crowbar.

I'm as tired as a little by gosh. And I'm near about past goin'.

This morning I got up so early that I met myself goin' to bed.

It's mighty hard for me to get goin'. I feel like I got one wheel down and was draggin' my axle.

I'm so blamed tired. I look like I was sent for and couldn't come.

"Your blind date was here to pick you up. I told him, 'She'll be right there as soon as she finishes shaving,' and before I could finish, he took off."

****

The soldier in Kuwait had been badly hurt by shellfire. A visitor stopped by his hospital bed and asked, "Were you hit by a shell, Soldier?"

He replied, "Nope. It crept up and bit me!"

****

"One thing you ought to know about that hospital. If you go there with high blood pressure, they'll keep you for two days, but if you have high insurance, they'll keep you for twenty!"

****

Harry Rogers was taken to his room in the hospital after the operation. He noticed that the window shades were drawn and the room quite dark. He asked the surgeon why the shades were drawn.

"There's a fire across the street, Harry, and I didn't want you to think the operation was a failure!"

The patient rang for his nurse, and, when she appeared in the doorway, he told her he wanted to see the chief cook.

"What on earth...Why in heaven's name would you want to talk to her?"

"Well, y'see, it's like this," the patient replied. "I want to ask her about this soup. Do I drink it or do I dip arrows in it!"

****

A woman talking about her friend in the hospital said, "She was so ill that they had to feed her inconveniently."

****

THE WHEEL CHAIR

The wheel chair, when it's self-propelled,
Can go as if bat-out-of-helled,
And with no sound of motor humming
Gives you no warning that it's coming.

On rubber tires, with spinning spokes,
It sneaks up on unwary folks,
On doctors, nurses, friends and foes,
And bashes rears and crushes toes.

Oh, cars and trucks are fierce on highways,
And so are bicycles in byways,
But in a dimly lighted corridor
The swift and silent wheel chair's horrider.

(*The Medical Muse*, by Richard Armour, 1963. McGraw-Hill Book Co. New York, NY. Reprinted with permission of Mrs. Kathleen S. Armour, Claremont, CA)

****

A person without a sense of humor resembles nothing so much as a wagon without springs...jolted by every pebble in the road.

****

In the men's bathroom of a Peoria, Illinois, hospital there is a sign that reads:
WARNING!
SCIENCE HAS PROVEN THAT
FLIES SPREAD DISEASE
KEEP YOURS BUTTONED!

In the ladies' room, there is this sign:
VYISDER ZOMENIMORE
ORZIZZAZIZ
ZANZARIS ORZIZ

IDEAL PATIENT

The perfect patient let us praise:
He's never sick on Saturdays,
In fact this wondrous, welcome wight
Is also never sick at night.
In waiting rooms he does not burn
But gladly sits and waits his turn,
And even, I have heard it said,
Begs others, "Please, go on ahead."
He takes advice, he does as told,
He has a heart of solid gold.
He pays his bills, without a fail,
In cash, or by the same day's mail.
He has but one small fault I'd list.
He doesn't (what a shame!) exist.

(*The Medical Muse*, by Richard Armour, 1963. McGraw-Hill Book Co. New York, NY. Reprinted with permission of Mrs. Kathleen S. Armour, Claremont, CA)

****

The retiring head of the State Street Memorial Hospital was attending the dinner given in his honor. At the conclusion of the meal, he was asked to say a few words. His speech went like this:

"Friends, when I came to this town forty years ago, I was jobless and unknown. I had only the clothes on my back and a few things wrapped in a red bandanna on a stick slung over my shoulder.

"Today, I am the general manager of this hospital, about to retire, and I own my own home, an office building, six fast food franchises here in town and a box factory."

After he had taken his seat, his friends gathered around him and one asked, "Jerry, what was in that red bandanna slung over your shoulder when you came to town?"

"As I recall," mused the old guy, "I had two hundred and fifty thousand dollars in cash and five hundred thousand in bonds!"

****

Did you hear about the hospital in Dallas, Texas, that was so swanky, so upscale that when you broke a bone they didn't merely set and bandage it...they set it and gift wrap it!

****

They say in Eureka, California, at the desk of the receptionist for the Six Rivers Planned Parenthood office, there is a sign that reads, "Contraceptionist."

Among the graffiti on a hospital bulletin board was this statement: "A researcher learns more and more about less and less until he knows everything about nothing."

****

"We're calling him 'Quits!'"

(Reprinted with permission of *Medical Economics*).

****

They've got to turn up the heat. Patients' rooms are colder than a witch's tit in a cast iron bra.

****

Typographical errors create some of the funniest and most accidental jokes.

These are some of the answers to questions researched by case workers handling applications for hospital service.

"Applicant says he has three children and a wife to boot."

"Applicant says her husband is paralyzed and can't make ends meet."

"Applicant says he has diabetes and is insulated twice daily."

"Applicant has trouble eating...has an ulster on his stomach."

Words Hospital Patients Don't Want to Hear

You know what a hospital room is. It's where friends of the patient go to talk to other friends of the patient. Never mind that the patient is gagging and turning blue. The visitors are going to discuss such things as the weather, taxes, the Busbee retirement pension, too much rain or the lack of it, income taxes, and "the time I had my operation."

I'll tell you, Dr. Kildare, here are a few things that, as a patient, you don't want to hear in your hospital room:

* "Well, I don't think he should buy any long-playing records."

* "It's a very rare disease. The only other time I've seen it is in a crossword puzzle."

* "I won't tell you where we found the skin to graft on your husband's chin, but occasionally his face may feel like sitting down."

* "We performed that operation just in the nick of time. Another few hours and you would have recovered without it."

* "What? Three thousand dollars for an exploratory operation on my wife? Forget it, I'll find out what's wrong with her at the autopsy."

* "I think my doctor used to be a veterinarian. He just told me to open my mouth and say, 'Moo.'"

* "Yes, we have to operate. My malpractice premium is due tomorrow."

* "Hmmmm, I thought they cured this years ago."

* "Down at the plant, they painted out your name in the parking lot this morning."

* "With this confounded new metric system, I can't figure out this thermometer. Either he has a temperature of 415 degrees or he's going eighty-five kilometers per hour."

* "If you're going to put money on today's football game, I suggest you bet only on the first half."

* "I wouldn't bother watching 'All in the Family' tonight. It's a two-parter."

* "Of course I wear a mask when I operate. That way, they're never sure who to blame."

And finally. . .

Doctor:　　"I can't find the cause of your liver trouble, Henry. But offhand, I'd say it was due to heavy drinking."

Patient:　　"I understand, Doc. Why don't I just come back when you are sober?"

All I Ever Wanted Was A Piece of Cornbread and A Cadillac, copyright 1989 by Bo Whaley and reprinted by permission of Rutledge Hill Press, Nashville, TN.

A soldier had been wounded and lay in a hospital bed. Two elderly ladies, on a comforting mission, stopped by his bed and noted the heavy bandaging of his head. "Oh, you poor dear," one of the ladies said. "Were you shot in the head?"

"No, Ma'am," the soldier replied. "I was shot in the foot and the bandage slipped up on me!"

****

Here are some definitions used to describe certain peculiarities in hospitals:

Zone of Quiet:	Where they break dishes morning, noon and night.
Sterilizer:	The germ's nemesis.
Wheel Chair:	Hospital taxi.
X-Ray:	Inside Information.
Bandage:	A cover that fits either too tight or too loose.
Blood Test:	A relic of the Spanish Inquisition.
Enema:	A washout.
Hospital:	A pain factory.
Ice Bag:	A non-addictive pain killer.
Laboratory:	The bug house.
Orderly:	Holder of an M.B. degree (Master of Bedpans).
Pyjamas:	Hospital tuxedo.

****

In the obstetrical department of a large New Orleans hospital, the physicians were surprised to find this sign posted: "LADIES READY-TO-BEAR DEPARTMENT."

****

It was determined that the sudden rush of patients hurt in traffic accidents could be attributed to the fact that they did not consider that the flow of pedestrian patients would be a lot less if there were more patient pedestrians.

****

Some good advice was handed out at a small hospital in Maryland. A poem was the form, and it went like this:

He heard the toot, but he surged to scoot,
And beat the choo-choo to it.
He wasn't sharp, now twangs a harp --
Make sure that you don't do it.

In the Illinois Medical Journal, more than forty years ago, they printed an interesting analysis of the ages of man, the stages each man goes through:

1. Milk.
2. Milk and bread.
3. Milk, bread, eggs, and spinach.
4. Oatmeal, bread and butter, green apples, and all-day suckers.
5. Ice cream soda and hot dogs.
6. Minute steak, fried potatoes, coffee, and apple pie.
7. Bouillon, roast duck, scalloped potatoes, creamed broccoli, fruit salad, divinity fudge, and demitasse.
8. Paté de foie gras, wiener schnitzel, potatoes Parisienne, egg plant à l'opera, demitasse, and Roquefort cheese.
9. Two soft-boiled eggs, toast, and milk.
10. Crackers and milk.
11. Milk.

(Perhaps they overlooked the final, but truly final, stage or "fix" for us all.)

12. Remission to the lay-away department.

(Reprinted with permission of the *Illinois Medical Journal*)

****

The poor man died in the hospital and his wife came into the room, looked down at her late husband and murmured, "Dear, sweet John. I sure do hope you've gone where I'm damned sure you ain't."

****

The man simply could not make it and died in hospital. But he had a good sense of humor and when they collected his things to take home, they found this little poem:

I like a lawyer, I even like
a good physician,
But one I can't and won't **stand** for is:
my neighborhood mortician.

****

Here's a first-class lesson in the progress of disease:

"Insignificant," said the soldier as he cut himself.
"Inattention," said the sergeant.
"Inflammation," said the hospital.
"Incurable," said the resident physician.
"Incredible," said the mourners.
"Interred," said his buddies.
"In peace," said his tombstone.

A woman, soon to give birth, came to the hospital for her final check-up. "Well, how's Oscar doing today?" the examining physician asked.

Obviously disturbed by his question, she snapped, "How did you know my coming baby's name was Oscar!"

"You mentioned it the last time you were in. I just wondered why you chose the name."

"I didn't. My husband named him Oscar because, he said, he represents the best performance of the year."

****

"Our lawyers are worried because it may get us into a patent infringement suit; but the staff is elated because it's speeded up circumcision 500 per cent."

(Reprinted with permission of *Medical Economics*)

****

Hospital Nursery: The bawl room.

****

He was a very large man and a new patient in the hospital. When they served him his first full-course dinner, he took one look at it and rang for the nurse. When she arrived, he yelled, "Nurse, at home there's more damned meat on the plate when I'm done eating than there is on this plate now!"

Nobody likes Doc Smith. He's about as popular in this hospital as a turd in a punch bowl.

****

New at her nursing studies, the flustered girl was instructed to wash her hands.

"Both of them?" she asked.

"No, just do the one," the head nurse replied. "I'm curious as to just how you'll get it done."

****

Here's a superb description of identical twins. "They look so much together, when they're apart you can't tell the two of them from both."

****

That little nurse is the fastest thing I've ever seen. She can get more work done in ten minutes than a dozen nurses can in an hour. She's faster than double-geared lightning! But you take Nurse Peters. Just the opposite! She's so slow she has to speed up to stop.

****

Patient to acupuncturist: "That's a jab well done!"

****

"I can find nothing wrong with you, Sir," the doctor told eighty-year old Eddie Jones. "You have the appearance of a man of forty years."

"It's not my appearance that concerns me, Doctor. It's my disappearance."

****

An old timer is one who can remember when bacon and eggs and sunshine were good for us.

****

The doctor entered the hospital room and asked the nurse, "And how is our patient's health? Heart action OK?"

"You bet, Doctor. This gent has propositioned me twice today."

It isn't often that a witty humorist and a poet with physical problems combines both conditions to create verse that combines the muse and the hospital. But Janet Henry did that in her collection, *Surviving the Cure.* Here are a few of her charming, revealing (and sometimes) excoriating poems based on her own serious illness.

HOSPITAL STAY

"We want to take you in for tests"
Sounds innocent enough.
I thought of bed-tray meals and rests
And all that pampered stuff.

I bought a pretty robe, to start,
Packed book and magazine.
And settled down to be a part
Of hospital routine. . . . . .

H
   E

      L

        P

Sip this, chew that, gargle, swallow.
   Breathe in, breathe out, focus, follow.

This side, that side, poke and probe.
   (So much for the pretty robe.)

Flex your muscles, make a fist,
   Bend your elbow, turn your wrist.

Veins for sticking, tubes for feeding.
   (So much for the leisure reading.)

Up and down and out and in,
   There's **no** place they haven't been!

   WHEW!

Home has never looked so good
Or family so dear.
Back to Wife-and-Motherhood;
I'll recover here.

Mastectomy

It hasn't changed my life style
And I haven't lost my touch.
The only thing I find is
I don't skinny-dip as much.

The Pusher

Here's a verse
For the Chemo Nurse:
Amen and Hallelujah!
It's very hard
To stay on guard
The way she slips it to ya!

Reverse Reaction

For years I fought my appetite
And lost with every meal.
And then I went on chemo pills
And food had no appeal.

At last I'd find the Thinner Me!
But something is the matter;
I'm eating less, enjoying less,
And only getting fatter.

Boo!

This is the drug that's
    giving me the rash.
And this one keeps me
    sporting a moustache.

With this one I am
    losing all my hair
And this one kind of
    bloats me here and there.

That's how these trick-or-treatments
    take their fee.
And every day is Halloween with me.

Off-Limits

Three of our daughters are experts
On cancer, its treatment and such.
They've been to some classes "for families"
And certainly learned very much.

I welcome advice on Resources,
And Help-that's-as-near-as-your-phone,
Nutrition, Self-Image and Sharing. . . . . .
But please leave my Sex Life alone!

Kindred Souls

Now and then it does me good
To have a conversation
With another patient in
My kind of situation.

It isn't very long before
The dialogue is humming
With ills and pills and doctor bills
And problems with our plumbing.

Hospital Gowns

"Take off your clothes and put on this"
Are words that shatter pride.
Soon there you are, all hanging out,
Without a place to hide.

The thing to do is ask for two,
(They always have a stack),
Then put on one to tie in front
And one to tie in back.

Then hope that
by some lucky chance
They'll let you
wear your underpants.

P.S.

And, entre-nous,
One thing's for sure;
The trick is to
Survive the cure.

"THE ONLY FOOLPROOF FORM OF BIRTH CON-
TROL IS ABSTINENCE? GREAT! WRITE
ME A PRESCRIPTION."

****

HEY NURSE, ARE YOU SENDING SOMETHING FOR MY IRREGULARITY?

3

DENTISTS

"Did you ever stop to think how lucky Adam and Eve were? They escaped teething." *(Mark Twain).*

****

There is only one class of males who can tell a woman to open up or shut up and that is...the dentist.

****

After a terribly busy day, Dr. Robert Coles, D.D., had a terrible night. He slept poorly and dreamed disturbing dreams during one of which he fought his pillow and chewed its insides out.

The next morning his wife, who had been disturbed at this restlessness asked, "Do you feel sick today, Dear?"

"Nope," he replied, "just a little *down* in the mouth."

****

A dentist with offices in a downtown building would leave a dime in the box of a poor man who sold gum in the lobby of the building. Every day for some years, the dentist would make this donation and never take the package of gum he was entitled to. One day, after the gift of a dime a day, the poor man said, "Doctor, I hate to tell you this, but the price just went up to 15¢."

****

I'm as old as my tongue and a little older than my teeth. *(Jonathan Swift, 1667-1745).*

****

Patient to dentist: "Doctor, do you know the way streaking began?"

Dentist: "I recently heard the answer to that. It seems a fellow picked up Bengay instead of Preparation H."

"I have just seen something that has made a believer out of me," the dentist told his dishonest assistant. "I really do believe, now, that there is life after death."

"Really? Tell me about it," replied his assistant.

"It was about an hour after you left yesterday to go to your Grandpa's funeral that he stopped in to see you."

****

A dentist at work in his profession always looks down in the mouth. *(George Prentiss, 1802-1870).*

****

Then there was the American guru in love with Hinduism who refused Novocain because he didn't believe in *Transcendental Medication.*

****

"Getting in any golf these fine days, Doctor?"

(Reprinted with permission from Dr. Gerald Epstein, *An Anthology of Dental Humor*)

Some doctors are absolute geniuses when it comes to common sense therapy. Consider the case of the dentist who called on this wise old doctor and complained of a terrible problem with insomnia. He just...couldn't sleep. "My suggestion, Dr. Brown, is that during the course of each day, you take four cups of wine."

"Will that make me sleep?" asked the dentist.

"I think so," was the reply. "But if it doesn't, it'll sure make you happy you're awake."

****

There is a certain literal-minded judge in Chicago who, when he swears-in a dentist, uses these words, "Do you swear to tell the tooth, the whole tooth and nothing but the tooth?"

****

"Doc, this tooth of mine is keeping me awake nights! Can you advise me?"

"Yep! Get yourself a job as a night watchman."

****

A man loses his illusions first, his teeth second, and his follies last. *(Helen Rowlan, born in 1871).*

****

Dr. Hugh Long, D.D.S., went to Colorado to learn to ski. He learned rapidly and had fun for a full week, but on the eighth day he was caught in an avalanche and was almost buried beyond help. He managed to work his way out of the deep, deep snow and into a tiny, deserted log cabin near the top of the mountain. There he stayed for two days, too weak to move and with nothing to eat. On the dawn of the third day, he heard a voice in the distance. "Dr. Long...Dr. Long," the voice called out. The cold, starved dentist stuck his head out the cabin window and called, "Who is it?" A voice came back, "The Red Cross."

"Oh, hell," Dr. Long yelled at him. "I already gave at the office."

****

You must have heard the one about the dentist who was driven to extraction.

Dr. Edward Pearson, D.D., placed this sign in his waiting room, "We know your children are a joy to behold. But please beholding on to them while in this waiting room."

****

"Mama, that dentist didn't tell the truth when he put that painless dentistry sign outside his door."

"Why do you say that, Dear?"

"Well he yelled just like any other dentist we've been to...when I bit his finger."

****

It is simply amazing how people get the facts all mixed-up. Consider the time at a dental conference where two old friends who hadn't seen one another in years, met. "Hey, Jack, glad to see ya, old buddy. I hear you hit it lucky...made two million bucks in Oklahoma oil, right?"

"Wrong. It wasn't Oklahoma, it was Texas. It wasn't oil, it was real estate. And it wasn't one million, it was three million...and I didn't make it, I lost it."

****

(*Sixth Over Sexteen*, J.M. Elgart, Editor)

There was a dentist named Booth,
Whose temper oft sent him through the roof.
    He said, "I must confide
    It scrapes off half my hide,
I'd rather be cleaning a tooth."

****

Some patients simply won't pay their dental bills. But this one dentist had a unique way of stimulating payments. He sent a bill with the following suggestion: I've been chasing after you to collect my bill for weeks! And I'm all out of breath:

We both need our money, I know I need mine.
I hope you get yours, that'd be fine.
But if you get yours and I don't get mine, too,
Just what in all hell am I going to do?

****

Doctor: "Nurse, you're late again!"
Dental Assistant: "Sorry, Doctor. It won't happen again because this morning I heard something that really opened my eyes. An alarm clock."

****

"The Doctor has a thing about garlic."

(Reprinted with permission from The Merritt Company, Santa Monica, CA)

"They still haven't invented a better set up!"

(Reprinted with permission from Gerald Epstein, D.M.D., *An Anthology of Dental Humor*, 1966)

****

A dentist called a plumber to fix a bad faucet. The job was done in twenty minutes.

"What's the bill?" asked the dentist.

"Seventy-five dollars," was the reply.

"What? That's banditry. I'm a dentist and I sure as hell don't make that kind of dough."

"I know, I know," said the plumber, nodding his head. "Neither did I back when I was a dentist."

****

The dentist's wife asked, "Have you noticed anything new about me, Dear?"

"Now that you mention it...yes...there is something new but I can't quite put my finger on what it is..."

"It's my breasts, Dear. Don't you think I look better without a brassiere?"

"Of course. That's it. Why, Dear, it has pulled all the wrinkles off your neck and face."

****

The patient slowly got up from the dental chair, rubbed his jaw and said, "Thanks, Doctor, and could I please have my bill?"

Dentist: "Not just yet. I don't think you are strong enough for that."

A dental school Professor of Dentistry, Dr. David Lewis, known everywhere for his long involved lectures, was suddenly brief and concise in the classroom. His students were quite puzzled by this radical change and one of them asked him why he had changed his method and length of lecture. "I happened to hear a remark passed by a couple of my students, following one of my lectures," Dr. Lewis explained, "and the one student said, 'I wonder who follows this speaker?' And the other student replied, 'Thursday!'"

****

The following statement on the bill a dentist sent to his few delinquent patients:

> Dear Sir: It seems to us, after noticing how very overdue you are in payment of your bill, that we have done more for you than did your mother. We have carried you for eighteen months.

****

*"You say you work for the
Internal Revenue Service?"*

(Reprinted with permission from Gerald Epstein, D.M.D., *An Anthology of Dental Humor*, 1966)

"All right, Mrs Tooks, I'm ready for Rodney now."

(Reprinted with permission from The Merritt Company, Santa Monica, CA)

****

Two friends met on the street, the one suffering from an excruciating toothache. "Howdy, Pete. Say...what's wrong? You look like you're standing on nails."

"It's this damned tooth of mine. Aches like hell. Don't know what to do about it. Got any suggestions?"

"Well, when I have a toothache that's bad as yours seems to be, why I go to my wife and ask for help. She just wraps her little arms around me, hugs and kisses me and pretty soon I forget all about the bad tooth. Why don't you try that?"

The other guy sighs, rubs his jaw and said, "Man, I sure do thank you for the suggestion. What's your address?"

****

There was actually a dentist's advertisement in a local paper that read:

TEETH EXTRACTED WITH THE
GREATEST PAINS

****

"Now tell me...which tooth hurts?" the dentist asked his patient.

"Well, Doctor...feels like the third row center, front row balcony," she replied, pointing to an upper cuspid.

When I finally got back to my home town, I called on all my old friends. One of them was my boyhood dentist, now old and grey, and I found him on his front porch, sitting and reading the Bible. "Just cramming for my finals," he said, grinning.

****

Perhaps one of the wittiest and most telling curses one man ever hurled at another was the one where he said, "All I want for you is that you should have all your teeth pulled except one...and in that one you should have the most gosh awful toothache man ever suffered."

****

Sometimes dentists are faced with insurmountable odds...in the form of patients who are about a pint short of a quart. Consider this:

A dentist had a patient afflicted with a bad case of Vincent's Angina. "I'll need a sample of your saliva," he told the patient.

"I ain't got none. Dad made me sell it all."

"I think you misunderstood. Please expectorate in this cup."

"I can't. I wan't never no good at athletics."

"Now look," shouted the exasperated dentist. "All I'm asking is that you spit in that cup on the window sill."

"Who me? From here?"

****

"Miss Bumsteer, how did you word that equipment order?"

(Reprinted with permission from The Merritt Company, Santa Monica, CA)

A dentist was faced with the biggest mouth he ever had seen. And when she opened it for him to begin work, he was astonished at the enormous cavern in front of him. "Thank you, Ma'am. That's wide enough. I plan to work outside it."

****

"Just tell him his partner is here."

(Reprinted with permission from The Merritt Company, Santa Monica, CA)

****

A dentist, young Doctor McBone,
Got a lovely girl patient alone.
And in his depravity filled quite the wrong cavity.
Ye gods, how his practice has grown!

****

An elderly couple was known for their parsimony. In fact, they were the cheapest, stingiest, savingest people in town. Well, they went to a restaurant and ordered one ham sandwich and two plates. The order griped the waiter, who knew all about them, but he filled the order. A bit later, he passed the table and noticed that the wife was eating but the husband's half of the sandwich lay untouched on his plate.

"Something wrong with your big, big lunch, Sir?" he asked contemptuously.

"Nope! Ever'thing's just fine. Only she's using our teeth."

126

NOTHING BUT THE TOOTH

Talkative factory workers develop carious teeth more readily than do silent ones, according to the British Dental Association.

--News Item.

Although the evidence is various,
They say that talkers' teeth are carious
More than the teeth of workers who
Just concentrate on what they do.

Could this be caused by more exposure
Of teeth to air? There's no disclosure
As yet, in what we've read, of whether
It's this, or banging more together.

Whatever are the latest guesses
Concerning this, the D.D.S.s,
It's clearly one more reason man
Should keep his mouth shut all he can.

(*The Medical Muse* by Richard Armour, 1963. McGraw-Hill Book Co. New York, NY. Reprinted with permission of Mrs. Kathleen S. Armour, Claremont, CA)

****

"Doctor, there's a rare book collector out here in the waiting room who's interested in some of our magazines."

(Reprinted with permission of The Merritt Company, Santa Monica, CA)

127

The American frontier was a fascinating, romantic place (at least in retrospect) but it was no place to have a toothache. Consider this witty *"Cure for the Toothache,"* in a *Farmer's Almanac* of 1857:

"Get a kettle of water -- let it come to a boil, then put your head into it and let simmer for precisely half an hour. Take out your head and shake all your teeth into a heap; pick out the decayed ones and throw them away. The sound ones you can put back again."

****

An ingenious dentist found a way to handle a particularly nervous old lady patient. She panicked regularly the moment she seated herself in his chair, and clamped her mouth so tightly that he couldn't pry it open. So one afternoon he had his girl assistant sneak up behind her, and as soon as he was ready to drill, she got the signal to jab the lady in the rear with a hatpin. She opened her mouth to holler -- and that was that.

His ministrations completed, the dentist consoled the patient, "Now that wasn't so bad after all, was it?"

"Not quite," the old girl admitted, still trembling, "but I certainly didn't expect to feel the pain so far down!"

****

"Tell me, Doctor, what can I do about bad breath?"

(Reprinted with permission from Gerald Epstein, D.M.D., An *Anthology of Dental Humor*, 1966).

DENTAL COLLEGE

"He's a good student, but his mind wanders."

****

An itinerant evangelist was exhorting his temporary congregation about the wages of sin, and the wrath to come: "Where you folks is goin', I warn all of ya, there is goin' to be wailin' and weepin' and gnashin' of teeth."

An old woman stood up: "Mister Parson, Suh, I ain't got no teeth."

"Madam, not to worry...teeth'll be provided!"

****

Orthodontist: A specialist who packs your mouth with certain metals while removing gold from your pocket.

****

A tourist in China came upon this sign outside a dentist's office:
    Insertion of false teeth.
    Latest Methodists.

"I find," said an old man to a BOOMERANG reporter, yesterday, "that there is absolutely no limit to the durability of the teeth, if they are properly taken care of. I never drink hot drinks, always brush my teeth morning and evening, avoid all acids whatever, and although I am 65 years old, my teeth are as good as ever they were."

"And that is all you do to preserve your teeth, is it?"

"Yes, sir; that's all -- barring, perhaps, the fact that I put them in a glass of soft water nights."

****

Old Rip Snorter was the biggest yellow "peerch" that had lived in the Wabash for a good many years. He had lived so long that his teeth had all fallen out, and he had gotten as gaunt and peaked as a grass-fed carp. It was a sad case, and it seemed as though the days of Old Rip were numbered.

One day Mrs. Browne was talking with a neighbor on the river bridge. Mrs. Browne was the proud possessor of a set of teeth which were like the lady villain's in the old-fashioned story -- beautiful but false.

The brisk breeze blowing over the river struck square between the shoulder blades of Mrs. Browne and made a ticklish sensation to stir in her nose.

"Ker-Bizz!" she sneezed, and those lovely teeth sailed out into the air, and dropped into the water with a mellow plunk.

Whenever Old Rip Snorter was seen after that, folks were surprised to see him so fat and flourishing. And just to add insult to injury, one day while Mrs. Browne was taking a boat ride, she saw Old Rip Snorter rise to the surface and grin at her, sassy as you please. And right then she recognized in his mouth her very own teeth that she had dropped when she sneezed long long before.

****

Dentist: "Quit making faces and squirming like that, Sir. I haven't begun on your tooth."

Patient: "I know that, Doctor, but you're standing on my sore toe."

****

"I sure caught hell from my wife for partying with the gang last night. What did your wife have to say?"

"Nothing. As a matter of fact, I was going to have these two front teeth pulled anyway!"

"The dentures are great—can't stop smiling...But I'm a mortician!"

(Reprinted with permission from Gerald Epstein, D.M.D., *An Anthology of Dental Humor*, 1966)

****

"Twenty bucks seems like a helluva price for pulling one lousy tooth. It only took a couple of seconds to do it."

"You should have told me you wanted me to extract it slowly...slowly."

****

Joe Copeland, D.D.S., was attempting a putt on the ninth hole when he saw a funeral procession moving past the golf course. He took off his cap, placed it over his heart and stood in silence until the procession had passed.

"That was very good of you, Joe," his partner said. "I didn't realize you were so sentimental."

"It was the very least I could do," Joe said, sinking his putt. "Just consider...next Wednesday would have been our thirtieth wedding anniversary."

In this day of specialization, the following story almost rings true. It seems that Hathaway Brown had a bad tooth and went to his dentist. The dentist deadened the nerve and began to work the tooth out. But he lost it just as it came out and the tooth dropped into his throat.

"Doggone it, can't help you now," the dentist exclaimed. "You've got to see a nose and throat specialist."

So Hathaway Brown high-tailed it to the nose and throat man, sat down in the chair a bit too abruptly and swallowed the tooth. "It's in your stomach," the specialist informed Hathaway. "You go to see an internist."

Well, at the internist's, an x-ray showed the tooth in the stomach. As the doctor fished for it with his special rod, the tooth left the stomach and lodged in the intestine.

"Dadblameit!" the specialist shouted. "Now you got to go see a proctologist because I handle only the stomach."

A few minutes later, the poor patient was undressed and in the examination room. "Bend over and I'll see what's up there," the proctologist told him. So Hathaway bent over, the doctor inserted the necessary instruments and then said, "By golly, you got a tooth up there, Mr. Brown. You'll have to see a dentist."

****

The phone rang in the dental office. The dentist picked up the phone and listened to a patient ask for an appointment that afternoon. "I'm sorry, I can't take you this afternoon," the dentist said, eyeing his golf bag, golf clothes and all, "because I have eighteen cavities to fill."

****

Dentist: "Nurse, I think this patient is regaining consciousness. He just tried to blow the foam off the mouthwash."

****

The dental surgeon completed a thorough examination on the pretty young thing, stepped back, shook his head and said, "Young lady, I dislike having to tell you this but...you have acute pyorrhea."

"Never mind the compliments, Doctor," she snapped. "Let's just get on with the examination."

****

Never mind losing all your teeth. Compensation there is. Now you can whistle while brushing your teeth.

"How does that sound for a collection letter?"

(Reprinted with permission from Gerald Epstein, D.M.D., *An Anthology of Dental Humor*, 1966).

****

Merchant: "Only yesterday, it seems, business was so good that I lit my cigars with $100 bills."
Doctor: "How extravagant of you."
Merchant: "Not really. It was a bill from my dentist and I wasn't figurin' on payin' him, anyway."

****

A dentist whose first name was Floss,
Fell in love with his nurse named Doss;
But he held in great hatred,
Her given name Gertrude,
So he called her his dear "Dental Floss."

****

"Mama, did you tell me that our new baby has your eyes and daddy's nose?"
"That's right, honey."
"Well, I got to tell you, Mom, you better be careful, 'cause he's got Grandpa's mouth."

A dentist placed the following sign immediately in front of his dental chair. It is not known if any patients took the advice literally.

Don't bother about how you're feeling
Cause a smile is great at healing.
It spreads like a wreath
'round front and back teeth,
And prevents the sore face from congealing.

****

A man slunk into the dentist's office with a towel wrapped from his jaw to the top of his head. Hardly any of his face could be seen.

"Holy smokes!" laughed the dentist. "I haven't seen that kind of a get-up bandage for thirty years. I take it you have a toothache?"

"Nope," the man replied. "You're wrong. This is a stickup!"

****

Dentists hold their looks and, seemingly, their age remarkably well. One of the best ways to tell if a dentist is aging is to watch him chase his nurse around the office. Stop him and ask him why he is doing this. If he can't remember why, well, then you know he's gettin' mi-i-ghty old.

****

Then there was the dentist who, while playing golf with his buddy, remarked that "it seems incredible that I could live with the same woman for 45 years. And if my wife finds out about it, she'll pull my tongue out by the roots."

****

Then there was the dentist who asked his wife what she'd like to have for her birthday.

"Tell you what," she said, "Why don't you give me something difficult to break...like a $1,000 bill."

****

A doctor's work fills a mere six feet of ground, but a dentist...ah...a dentist's work fills an entire acher.

A man walked into the optometrist's office and told him, "Doctor, I'm in serious trouble. It's getting so I can't tell heads from tails."
"I take it you are a gambler or work in a coin exchange?"
"No, Doctor, it's worse than that. I'm a dentist."

****

(Reprinted with permission from The Merritt Company, Santa Monica, CA)

****

The dentist was reading a technical medical paper at a national convention. But when he came to the ending line, he read, "The patient developed a history of being consonated for seventy-two hours."
From the audience, a kindly voice responded, "Doctor, I think you mean constipated and not consonated, did you not?"
"You are right, Doctor. I've a new denture and have been having trouble moving my vowels."

****

As Charlie McCarthy used to say..."I've got a tooth that's driving me to extraction."

135

ODE TO THE RETIRED DENTIST
(A Parody on Longfellow's "Psalm of Life")

Tell me all your troubles,
Life is but an empty dream,
But when you're retired as a dentist,
Oh! how happy life doth seem!
But life is real, when you do things right,
And labor hard from morn 'til night.
When your harvest days are over,
And your Florida nights are spent,
With your forceps old and rusty,
And your drills, some broke, some bent,
You will near the gates of Heaven,
But inside you'll never get.
For Saint Peter there will tell you,
"We've no retired dentists in here yet."

****

Dr. Edward Gossens, D.D., had worked hard all his life with few vacations. When asked why he worked so hard, he replied, "Hard work is the yeast that raises the dough."

****

This "Ode to a Dental Hygienist" was given by Earnest Albert Hooton, Harvard professor of Anthropology, as the peroration of his address to the graduating class of dental hygienists at the Forsyth Dental Infirmary in July 1942.

Hygienist, in your dental chair
I sit without a single care,
Except when tickled by your hair.
I know that when you grab the drills
I need not fear the pain that kills.
You merely make my molars clean
With pumice doped with wintergreen.
So I lean back in calm reflection,
With close-up views of your complexion,
And taste the flavor of your thumbs
While you massage my flabby gums.
To me no woman can be smarter
Than she who scales away my tartar,
And none more fitted for my bride
Than one who knows me from inside.
At least as far as she has gotten
She sees how much of me is rotten.

DENTIST DEFINITIONS

A PRESTIDIGITATOR WHO, PUTTING METAL IN YOUR MOUTH, PULLS COINS OUT OF YOUR POCKET.

A MAN WHO LIVES FROM HAND TO MOUTH

A MAN WHO RUNS A FILLING STATION

A COLLECTOR OF OLD MAGAZINES

(Reprinted with permission from The Merritt Company, Santa Monica, CA)

****

It seems as though the older a man gets, the more convinced he becomes that Mother Nature is scheming against him for the benefit of doctors and dentists.

****

The nervous patient in the waiting room was about to leave from all the shouting and swearing he heard coming from the dental operating room.

Suddenly the nurse opened the door and said to him, "Don't let all that hell and damnation and blasphemy bother you, Sir. It's just that the minister is trying out his new teeth by repeating last Sunday's sermon."

SONG IN A DENTIST'S CHAIR
(Which I Wish Someone Would Set to Appropriate Music)

All joys I bless, but I confess
    There is one greatest thrill;
What the dentist does when he stops the buzz
    And puts away the drill.

His engine hums along my gums
    Its excavating drone,
I salivate and gurgling wait
    Vibrating to the bone.

Oh, will he save this tooth concave
    Or will he new decide
To grind away some more decay?
    He murmurs, *Open wide.*

So I must feel the burring steel,
    The hot and fragile twinge,
And mutely bide till he push aside
    The bracket on its hinge.

But will he swerve across that nerve?
    I wonder, gagged, agape;
He sees me gulp and spares the pulp --
    My God, a close escape!

The creosote is in my throat,
    I weep against my will;
My nostrils itch, sensation which
    I can't relieve until
He stops the buzz and packs in fuzz
    And puts away the drill.

I grant the bliss of love's warm kiss
    Or wealth, or fame, or skill;
These I esteem but yet I deem
    There is one greater thrill --
When he stops the buzz, as at last he does,
    And puts away the drill!

****

"Hey, dammit, Doc, that wasn't the tooth I wanted you to pull."
"I know, I know. Hold your horses...I'm coming to it."

There is one thing certain in this world. Whether or not you have teeth matters not in the least, when you smile, because a smile never goes up in price or down in value.

****

Edgar Jeffries had just come to Springfield, Illinois, and he was looking to establish necessary contacts to begin his new life. He asked an associate for the name of a good dentist. Given the name, he then asked if the man was truly good at his profession.

"Well," the friend answered, "not more than a couple of years ago I went to that dentist and had a lot of work done. Then, about a week ago, I was playing a game of golf when the fellow behind me hit a drive and that damned ball caught me right in the groin. I tell you that for the first time since that dentist finished with me, my teeth stopped hurting!"

****

IMA N. PAINE, DDS

"YOU SHOULD'VE THOUGHT OF THAT BEFORE YOU GOT INTO DENTISTRY, IMA."

****

It is a dental truism that all dental patients need to learn and never forget: Never, never leave the dentist's chair until you are strong and steady enough to face the cashier.

The dentist's wife was known as the cheapest, most frugal penny-pincher in town. Well, as it must to all men, death approached the dentist and his last words to his wife were: "Dear, all I want for my funeral is that you put on my coffin a nameplate."

"I'll do it, Dear," she promised. And the dentist closed his eyes in death.

On the morning of the funeral, at the cemetery, when the coffin was unloaded from the undertaker's vehicle, there, plain and obvious for all to see, was the nameplate. It read:

EDWARD STEVENS, D.D.S.
OFFICE HOURS 10 to 5

****

At a dinner party, one of the guests was having trouble with his steak. The fellow next to him noticed his trouble, saying, "That steak looks kind of tough...like the kind that insists on mooing."

"No, it's not the steak. It's my teeth. They keep slipping around in my mouth."

"I believe I can help you." The man reached into his pocket, saying, "Here, try this set." But that one didn't fit either. So he pulled out a couple more and one of them fit just fine. "Say this set is just great," the troubled man said. "But how come you had so many sets of teeth with you? You must be a dentist."

"Nope. Merely an undertaker."

****

It's true that there are not many jokes circulating about dentists. Maybe the reason is that getting them to say something funny is about like pulling teeth.

****

The old French Canadian had reached the astonishing age of one hundred and ten. A reporter came to his home to interview him for an article in the newspaper. "Francoise, to what do you attribute your wonderful old age?" the reporter asked.

"Wine, son," the old man said. "I never touched a drop of water. Only wine has ever passed my lips because water is harmful."

"But what about things like...well, like brushing your teeth. You must have used water for that?"

"Never. For that I use a light sauterne."

(Reprinted with permission from Gerald Epstein, D.M.D., *An Anthology of Dental Humor,* 1966)

A man and his wife entered the dentist's office and at once the woman announced, "I want to have this tooth pulled, Doctor, and never mind drugs or gas or any pain killer. We got to get it done and get out of here."

"Very well, Madam, follow me. And I must say that you have great courage, Madam."

"Henry," his wife said, turning to him, "show him your tooth."

****

The dentist told the patient that her tooth would have to come out at once. Further, he recommended a certain oral surgeon for the job.

The patient left and went immediately to the oral surgeon, who seated her in his operating room, then prepared for the extraction.

As the surgeon reached into her mouth, the patient moved her hand to a very vulnerable part of his anatomy, just below his belt.

"What the hell are you doing!" he yelled.

"Don't worry," the patient said. "So long as you don't hurt me, I won't hurt you."

****

There was an old fellow named Reeth,
Who forgot where he laid his false teeth,
    They were set on a chair,
    He'd forgot they were there,
He sat down and was bit underneath.

****

Here's a funny account of an occurrence at an American Dental Convention that took place in 1873. Back then they were not entirely in favor of all those newfangled dental innovations that were happening. The discussion was about a new technique, *amalgam,* and a dentist had demonstrated the new technique of amalgam filling. Then another dentist, Dr. Teeters, stood and delivered this rebuttal:

"It is my earnest conviction that any dentist who...uses such a relic of barbarism as the combination of quicksilver and ironfilings, known to the profession as 'amalgam'...deserves himself to be drilled just back of the ear with one of those infernal buzz-saws lately introduced into dentistry under the name of 'mechanical drills,' have the cavity scraped with a coal-shovel, and to be finally 'plugged' with a set of forceps shot from a musket."

Foley's Footnotes: A Treasury of Dentistry by Gardner P. H. Foley.

These observations by Alexander Edwin Sweet, in his book, *Texas Siftings,* 1882, offer interesting observations of the dental profession, a journalist's view of it, more than a century ago.

THE DENTIST

Readers who are squeamish about pain, and scenes of torture, and dental repair, should be warned against reading the following article. It ought to keep them away from regular check-ups forever.

The modern dentist is not like the dentist of long ago. The old time dentist did not repair teeth; he simply uprooted those that were decayed. It is only of late years that the dentist has occupied a recognized position in the departments of minor surgery. Some dexterity and considerable muscular strength were the chief qualifications of the dentists of our childhood. When a patient called on one of them, the dentist would put his finger in the patient's mouth, and after feeling around among the stumps and shaking them one after another until a howl from the patient demonstrated that he had hold of the right one, he would say, laconically, "It's got to come out." Then he would go for his instruments. These mechanical appliances were of a very primitive character. They consisted of several pairs of things like bullet moulds; those of the largest size he used on adults, and the small ones on children. While he was engaged filing the rest of his instruments, the sufferer had time to note the contents of the room. On a shelf was a rope, with which nervous patients were tied in the operating chair; on another chair a basin, and a pitcher with a broken handle, containing water presumably for the purpose of washing away such gory evidences of butchery as the operation might leave; on a broken-legged desk, propped with a brick, was a skull with a cracked jaw bone, which was too suggestive to be pleasant or soothing; in the window sill the dentist's library consisting of a copy of Wedl's *Pathology of the Teeth,*[1] and a portion of a volume of Moore's melodies;[2] in front of the operating chair, hanging on the wall, was a steel engraving representing Napoleon on the Island of St. Helena. The picture was evidently put there with the view distracting the patient's attention from thoughts of the agony in store for him. While he was wondering if Napoleon ever had a toothache, and if he ever burned the inside of his mouth with creosote and oil of cloves in his efforts to deaden the pain; and while he was wishing that he could change places with Napoleon for a day or two, the dentist grasped him by the hair, threw his head back, inserted the can opener in his mouth, and began groping around for the bad tooth. When he found it, his usual plan was to crush it into pieces and dig out the fragments, one at a time. During the operation the sufferer groaned, and moaned, and yearned for death. When the dentist got his grappling irons around the root of a double tooth, and braced himself with his foot against the wall for a long pull, a strong pull, and a pull all together, the patient thought that the end of all things was at hand, that an explosion had occurred in the cellar, and that the heavens were rolling themselves up as a scroll, while the top of his head was being broken off, and his vertebra was being jammed down into the hollow of his legs. When he was calmed with a glass of water he found that the alarming sensations he had experienced were caused, as the dentist put it, by "the extraction of the molar from the alveolar cavity."

The modern dentist is a different kind of an aggravated outrage. He has a college diploma that he keeps hanging on the wall in a tin case. He usually has a nicely furnished operating room, where he has an elaborate chair, working on pivots and hinges, that he places the patient in when he is pulling his tooth, and another to be used when a tooth is being filled. He has hundreds of instruments -- diminutive augers and gouges and scrapers,[3] and one vile thing that seems to make about seven hundred revolutions to a minute, and with which he bores into the nerve of your tooth until you feel as if your immortal soul was being tampered with. But the modern dentist seldom pulls a tooth. He prefers to fill it with some gutta percha sort of composition, or with gold. You see, the filling will, in the course of time, come out and then he gets another job putting it in again, whereas when he pulls out a tooth that ends it; the owner of the tooth seldom cares to have it decorated, or to squander bullion on it after it is out. He usually carries it in his vest pocket for two or three days, and then throws it into some vacant lot. When a man has an aching tooth that tries to push itself into prominence, that seems to swell up and get in the way of everything he eats, and to take more of his thought and attention that he can spare, he can go to the modern dentist, who will fill him up with gas until he imagines he is a balloon, soaring up almost as high as the dentist's charge for the operation, and when he comes to earth again, the tooth will be gone and there will be a vacant place in his jaw that will seem to be about the size of a town lot. The painless dentistry of to-day is less exciting than the painful dentistry of the past, but it is otherwise an improvement on the old style.

1.   Carl Wedl, a German Dentist, wrote *Pathology of the Teeth* in 1871. The English translation was published in 1872 and republished in 1873 by the Philadelphia publishing house of Lindsay and Blakiston *(National Union Catalogue: Pre-1956 Imprints).*
2.   *A Selection of Irish Melodies,* by poet Thomas Moore, contained such songs as "Believe Me, If All Those Endearing Young Charms" and "The Last Rose of Summer" (Michael Stapleton, comp., *The Cambridge Guide to English Literature,* pp. 614-615).
3.   According to a Galveston dentist, augers were used for drilling, gouges to remove roots, and scrapers to clean teeth.

4

NURSES

Just out of bed for the first time, the new mother dressed in her robe and walked down the hospital corridor to the telephone. She asked for a directory and was busily thumbing through it when her nurse came by. "What are you doing out here, for heaven's sake," the nurse exclaimed.

"I'm searching through the phone book for a name for my baby," the new mother replied.

"You don't have to do that here. The hospital furnished a booklet to all new mothers. It's got every first name you could think of."

"You don't understand," she said and frowned. "My baby already has a first name."

****

There was a cute nurse from Centralia,
Who went to a dance as a dahlia.
    When the petals uncurled,
    It revealed to the world,
That the dress, as a dress, was a failure.

****

A good appetite needs no sauce.

****

Someone described laughter as being quite similar to changing a baby's diaper. The action doesn't solve any serious problems but, for a time, it makes things a whole lot more agreeable.

****

People who know, say that God's favorite music is laughter.

****

There was an old nurse from Minn.
Who was so desperately thin,
    That when she assayed,
    To drink pink lemonade,
She slipped through the straw and fell in.

There is this new kind of hang-up called male chauvinism. This joke appeared long before the term entered general usage:

Nurse in mental hospital: "Doctor, there's a man on the phone who wants to know if any of our patients have escaped recently."

Doctor: "Why on earth does he want to know such a thing?"

Nurse: "He said somebody has run off with his wife."

****

There was a patient in the hospital who was so nasty and despicable that the nurses all sent him "get well" cards.

****

"YES, YOU DID HEAR ME REFER TO YOU AS A 'V.I.P.!' — A 'VERY INCORRIGIBLE PATIENT'.

****

Nurse Dobbins came home to her husband and she was wearing a spankin' brand new uniform with a very short skirt and low bodice. Her husband took one look and said, "Honey, I just purely do love that new uniform of yours."

"Sho' nuff?"

"Wow! Sho' do."

146

The trouble with health foods is that you have to be strong as Sampson to unscrew the lids.

****

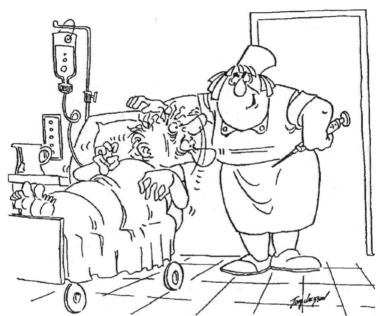

"You little nuisance you, guess what? We ran out of sleeping tablets."

****

Doctor: "Of course, Nurse Thomas had every right to be insulted at what you said. And I don't much blame her for belting you over the head for insulting her before she used the hypodermic. Just remember this maxim, 'Never insult an alligator until after, repeat, **after** you've crossed the river.'"

****

George Bernard Shaw, the great British philosopher, was a committed vegetarian. When he met Alfred Hitchcock, of blimp proportions, the latter remarked, "To look at you, G.B., one would really think there was a famine in England."
And the witty Shaw replied, "One would think you had caused it."

147

Constipation: To Have And To Hold.

****

"No, no, it's not a suppository, just a mod candle a visitor left while you were asleep."

****

The psychiatric nurse said she considered the world to be like a fruit cake...incomplete without a few nuts in it.

****

It happened at the University of Texas School of Medicine, so you know it must be true if it came from Texas.

In the psychopathic ward, Mr. E., a paretic patient, was having fever therapy in the heated box. Because he was so unruly and violent, they found it necessary to tie his hands to his sides. A nurse applied a thermometer in his rectum to note the temperature, then she left the room. When she came back in the room, she discovered the thermometer was...in...his...mouth. "How on earth did you get that thermometer in your mouth?" she gasped.

And here are the patient's exact words: "I burped."

A strange, rather wild-eyed patient approached the receptionist nurse in Chicago's Rush Hospital. "What can I do for you, Sir?" the nurse asked.

"I got a bad ankle," the patient explained. "Paul Revere came arunin' right at me and I sprained it when I jumped out'n his way. Been hurtin' ever since."

"Really?" the nurse replied, grinning at the notion. "And how come you managed to escape the Fort Dearborn massacre?" she asked, eyes atwinkle.

"I never missed it a'tall," said the odd one. "Why I saved my life by hiding among the cattails along the shore of Lake Michigan."

The nurse had had about enough and said sharply, "Let's get down to business, Sir! If you were half as old as you say you are you'd be pushing up daisies. The next thing you'll be telling me...you knew Noah, the ark builder!"

"By golly," the loony replied, "glad you brought that up. That sucker ain't never brought back my hammer."

****

Someone posted a sign in Mercy Hospital that read: "Interns think of GOD, Residents pray to GOD, Doctors talk to GOD, Nurses are GOD."

****

Worry is like a treadmill. It can wear you down to a nubbin' and yet not get you anywhere.

****

There was one doctor that the nurses all considered a prime pain in the...well...sit-down spot. Nurse Scroggins described him in this way, "I'd like to buy him for what he's worth and sell him for what he *thinks* he's worth."

****

One old joke that must go back to the Civil War has four nurses talking about how they got even with a doctor they considered an arrogant jerk. "I stuffed cotton in the bottom of his stethoscope," one nurse said. "What a time he's gonna have with patients tomorrow morning."

"And I let the mercury out of his thermometers and painted them all to read 106 degrees."

"Boy, did I get even with the old bastard," said the third nurse. I opened his desk drawer and found his box of condoms. WELL..., I punched a pinhole in every one of them."

The fourth nurse fainted.

Miss Edwards, the new nurse, was really inept, making all kinds of outrageous blunders with hypodermic needles, thermometers, bedpans, and the like. But she was determined to excel at her job.

One morning, the doctor in charge of her ward was shocked to see a patient running like crazy down the hall, yelling wildly, his gown streaming out behind him. Nurse Richards was running after him while holding a basin of steaming water.

"Stop, Nurse! Hey, there, stop, Nurse Edwards," yelled the doctor. "I told you to prick his boil, not...."

****

"Where IS the boil?"

(*Sixth Over Sexteen*, J. M. Elgart, 1956)

****

Einstein Made Understandable:

There was a young nurse named of Bright,
Whose speed was fastern'n light.
    She set out one day,
    In a relative way,
And returned the previous night.

Doctor: "Nurse, how is that little boy, the patient in 334, who swallowed a quarter last night?"
Nurse: "No change yet."

****

Nurse Evans was about to be married. She went to her psychiatrist and asked what she should do to have a happy life in marriage. He told her: "To be happy in or out of marriage, it is necessary that you live each day as if it were the first day of your honeymoon and the last day of your period."

****

The wife was in the delivery room and the husband was pacing the floor outside, wringing his hands, sighing and groaning. "Oh, the dear girl is so delicate. She is too fragile for this."
At last a nurse appeared. He ran to her saying, "Is she all right? My poor delicate wife?"
"Oh, yes. She's fine."
"Tell me," he groaned. "Is it a boy?"
The nurse looked at the distraught husband's face and said: "The middle one is."

****

Then there was the vegetarian nurse who refused to eat unless she got an increase in celery.

****

Did you ever know Nurse Treest?
She lived entirely on yeast.
        Said, "To me it's plain,
        We must all rise again --
And I want a headstart at least."

****

Nurse Jenny Posco advised her patients as follows: "Don't put aside laughter. Remember, there's no time like the pleasant."

****

I wonder how Mary makes it over at Memorial Hospital. She don't know "sic 'em" from "come here."

| Old Patient: | "Nurse, is there anything worse than being old and bent?" |
| Young Nurse: | "Yes, there is...being young and broke." |

****

The nurse who can smile when things go wrong is probably going off duty.

****

A young nurse named Mary Maureen,
Grew so very remarkably lean.
    So flat and compressed,
    That her back touched her chest,
And sideways, she couldn't be seen.

****

There was a cute nurse from Delent,
Who said she knew what it meant
        When guys asked her to dine,
        Gave her whiskey and wine.
She knew what it meant -- but she went!

****

HOLD EVERYTHING

Children wiggle,
        Children squirm.
Ever try to
        Hold a worm?

Children fidget
        While you work.
Just get set,
        And children jerk.

****

Offices,
        Though well equipped,
Need one thing,
        I say, tight-lipped:

Nothing else
        Would be so nice
Or so useful
        As a vice.

(*The Medical Muse* by Richard Armour, 1963. McGraw-Hill Book Co. New York, NY. Reprinted with permission of Mrs. Kathleen S. Armour, Claremont, CA)

Not all nurses and student nurses, RNs or whatever, are case examples of brilliant brains. Here are some descriptions of nurses -- heard around hospitals -- sayings having to do with stupidity, absent-mindedness, or just plain dumbness.

She was born stupid and she's been losing ground ever since.

Smart? Hardly! If her brains were black ink, she couldn't find enough to dot an "i."

When the good Lord was passing out brains, she thought He said "trains" and got out of the way.

She's six pickles short of a barrel.

She's so stupid, so derned dumb, that she couldn't locate her own butt with both hands, a compass and a flashlight.

****

(Sixth Over Sexteen, J. M. Elgart, 1956)

****

A young nurse had recently completed her tests for a driver's license. She took her final practicals, driving with a state policeman, and proceeded to drive right on through a red light.

"Young lady," inquired the cop, "What does a red light mean to you?"

Without hesitation she replied, "A bedpan!"

A patient in the mental hospital was observed swaying from side to side, much like a pendulum.

"Are you exercising?" the nurse asked.

"No, I'm keeping time," the patient replied.

"I see. Hm-m. So tell me...what time is it?"

"Three-thirty."

"Sorry, you're wrong," said the nurse, looking at her watch. "It's now four o'clock."

"Holy smokes!" exclaimed the patient. "I'll just have to sway a bit faster."

****

Marilyn Edgars trained hard to be a nurse and was graduated with honors. Then she got married, had a child, then another, then another and rarely had time to practice her profession. Her husband died but Marilyn soon married again. After four children, the second husband passed away leaving Marilyn with seven kids. tough going, and she needed to take up her profession. But home duties made the practice of nursing quite sporadic.

Then Marilyn married again and had two more kids and again became a widow. Shortly after the death of her husband, Marilyn died. Two of her classmates came to the funeral home to pay their respects. As one nurse looked down at the body, she shook her head, saying: "It's a good to know they're together now."

"Yes," responded her companion, nodding. "It is good that she is now with all three husbands."

"I was referring to her knees," said the first nurse.

****

The patient in Room 623 called to a nurse: "Nurse, come here, please." And the nurse entered his room. "Nurse, I got to ask you a question about this new diet they put me on when I get out of here."

"Sure, ask ahead. I'll try to answer your questions," the nurse said.

"Well, tell me this. They took me off bread. Won't let me eat a danged slice of it. So tell me...how in hell am I supposed to sop up the gravy?"

****

"I hear what you're saying," the head nurse remarked to the complaining male nurse. "I understand just what you mean when you feel dog-tired at the end of the day. Well, young man, may I suggest that the reason for feeling that way is because you've done nothing but growl all day."

The patient had just returned home from a stay at the hospital where she was operated on for hemorrhoids. Her sister came in to see her. "Was the operation a success, Dear?" sister asked.

"Yes, I guess so," the bedded patient replied. "But it sure does worry me."

"Worry? But you said it was a successful operation, didn't you?"

"It was. But I'm afraid that for the rest of my life, it'll be an eyesore."

****

The head nurse was about to address a mixed group of recently graduated nurses, both male and female. She looked over the name list of the group, frowned, and asked, "Attention please. Do we have a Peter Period here?"

A male voice from the rear replied, "No, Nurse, we don't. We hardly have time for a coffee break!"

****

One cute nurse confided to her friend that she had kissed almost every doctor in the hospital.

"Interns?" her friend asked.

"No," was the response...."Alphabetically."

****

Doctor:	"Do you know the one word that a nurse ought to learn early and use regularly?"
Nurse:	"No!"
Doctor:	"That's right."

****

Then there was the nurse who was sent by a surgeon to procure sutures. "Are these 10-day or 20-day sutures?" the doctor asked.

The nurse replied, "Darned if I know how old they are, Doctor."

****

There is an old story about the nurse who kept going to the supply room for a bedpan. After she'd made several trips, the attendant asked, "Nurse, what on earth are you doing with all those pans?"

"Well, there's this foreign patient in 392 who, every time I stick my head in his room and ask if all is OK, he tells me 'wee, wee.' So I get him another bedpan."

"NURSE!"

(Reprinted with permission from *The Saturday Evening Post*).

****

Time To Rise
A birdie with a yellow bill
Hopped upon his window sill
Cocked his shining eye and said
"Aren't you 'shamed, you sleeping head?"

That was no birdie's jaundiced bill
But just a nurse who aids the ill,
Who waits until you're in a dream
To wake you with her morning scream.

(Bedside Manna, *"The Third Fun in Bed Book"* by Frank Scully, Simon & Schuster, 1936)

****

A most capable nurse in Bement,
Had a nose most awfully bent,
    She followed her nose
    Where it pointed, I s'pose -
But no one knows which way it went.

"Nurse," the doctor cautioned her, "watch your language. One of these days, you're going to get caught in your own mouth trap."

****

The *Pan American News Letter* is a joke sheet of puns published by the most beautiful and talented punsteresses in the entire nation. Here are a few of their voluminous offerings (or is it offsprings)?

1. He died from radiation...what a way to glow.
2. Many a person falls for the bellyhoo of diet foods.
3. The exotic dancer got a bad cold. It developed into a *strip* throat and she *barely* recovered.
4. Absinthe is said to be an aphrodisiac. One reason: absinthe makes the *tart* grow fonder.

****

It may be unfair, but here's a telling joke:
Mrs. White visited her friend in the hospital and was upset when she saw her ring the bell, to order drinks for her.
"But I'm not ringing for drinks," the patient responded. "This bell is supposed to bring the night nurse and I always ring it when I want a half-hour without interruption!"

****

Sometimes you wonder about a patient, whether he's got a full box of cookies. Consider the case of the fellow in Room 298 who was given a bath in bed by his nurse...but not quite all over. She handed him the washrag and said, "You know what you can do with this."
A bit later, in telling his buddy about the incident, he remarked that he really hadn't known what the nurse meant when she gave him the washrag. "But I thought I knew," he said. "And I got to tell you this...for the balance of my time there, I had the cleanest, shiniest windows in the whole blamed hospital."

****

The ancient nurse had worked in the same hospital for twenty-five years. "And since I've been here," she said, "over all those years, I've brought bedpans to twenty thousand nine hundred and forty-eight patients."
"My goodness," the hospital's administrator said, "How on earth did you get that figure?"
"I eat too damned much."

Back in the days of Elvis, bob and crazy pelvises, two nurses were observing a dissection. The physician in charge intoned the various parts of the interior of the cadaver: "Here you see the liver," he pointed out, "and this is the spleen and over here are the kidneys..."

"Wow! Man!" whispered the one young nurse to the other, "dig that crazy organ recital."

****

Two cute nurses were late getting to the hospital after a night on the town. They met two interns just going out the door. "Shh!" one nurse said. "We're slipping in after hours!"

"That's fine," replied one of the interns. "We're slipping out after ours."

****

An intern was in competition for the hand of a beautiful nurse. "I know I haven't got much now, Dear," the intern begged, "but I still want you to marry me."

"But we'll have nothing to live on except my salary," she replied, "and you know how little I make."

"Sure, I know," the intern importuned, "but something is bound to come along."

"You bet it will," she replied. "And when it does, how'll we ever feed it."

****

"I tell you, Mary," Nurse Sally said, "that patient in 462 just never quits talking. All day long, she keeps on blabbing. Seems like her tongue is tied in the middle and loose at both ends."

****

"Now you be real careful when you go before that examining board," her friend advised. "I know you want that job as head nurse in Pediatrics, but you be careful what you say. You be careful as a prostitute at confession."

****

Here lies the body of a cantankerous nurse Kay,
Who demanded she be given the right-of-way,
    She was dead, dead right as she walked along
Just as dead as if wrong, dead wrong all along.

"Miss Brandon," the doctor said to her as she appeared in his office, ready to work. "You've got to be more careful about your personal appearance if you want to continue in this office as nurse. Why, when you walked in the door this morning, I thought you looked like you tossed your clothes in the air and then ran under them!"

****

Nurse Perkins had been recently divorced and her best friend asked her, one day, a personal question. They were having coffee in the hospital cafeteria. "He seemed like such a nice fellow, Susie. How come you divorced him?"
"In some ways, he was a real nice guy," Nurse Perkins replied. "But to be perfectly honest with you, he was no more use to me than a needle without an eye."

****

"Did you know Mary Elins?" a nurse asked her friend. "She nursed at Maple Hospital in Urbana."
"Of course, I knew her. Swell gal. I've known her for, let's see now, I guess I've known her since at least fifty pounds ago."

****

When patients approached the discharge time from hospital, Nurse Edith Schoen used to prescribe for them in this way: "Just remember this, when your future seems *black*," she would say, "and you really have the *blues*, see *red* when your enemies bug you, or feel *green* with envy at somebody, then it's sure as heck time to *color your life with laughter.* And if you'll live that way, you'll end up feeling in the *pink.*"

****

There was a bold nurse so benighted,
She never knew when she was slighted;
    And out at a party,
    She'd eat plenty hearty,
As if she'd been really invited.

****

A wise nurse, now nearing seventy years of age, put it beautifully: "It's sure true that love makes the world go round...but it's laughter that keeps us from getting dizzy."

Above the desk of the station for nurses on the OB floor, there hung a sign: "USE YOUR HEAD...IT'S THE LITTLE THINGS THAT COUNT!"

****

Nurse Kann had been working with a patient suffering acute diarrhea. She left the room for a break and went to the coffee shop where a friend told her, "Mary...you smell like you want to be left alone."

****

You can't beat the Bible for wisdom. Laughter occupies a large place in that Book. For example, the Book of Ecclesiastes says, "A merry heart doeth good like medicine."

****

"MUST YOU JOT RECIPES ON MY PRESCRIPTION BLANKS? MR. HIGGINS'S DRUGGIST MADE HIM UP A MEAT LOAF!"

(Reprinted with special permission of King Features Syndicate)

****

It was reported that the Mayo Clinic in Arizona, when questioned about potential danger in using decaffeinated coffee, replied that such fears were *groundless.*

The *Pun American Newsletter* published puns devised by members of the organization. Here are a few from this great group headquartered at 1185 Elmwood Place, Deerfield, IL 60015:

At the municipal hospital cafeteria in Deerfield, Illinois, they serve sandwiches with the following distinguished names:

Ava-Dada Deal For You
Ham Dunk
The Swallows of Capastrami
Twenty Thousand Livers Under The Cheese
Bagel Borrow and Steal
Keystone Cobbs
Lox O'Luck
Sylvester Stalami

Then these wily punsters go on to talk of the near-sighted nurse whose favorite sport was riding on "A Bi-focal Built For Two."

They also suggest the favorite love song of an alcoholic: "I Get A Hic Out Of You."

****

Then there was the nurse in Dermatology who described her bosses as "A Hive of Allergists."

****

At nursing school, male nurses were advised to never end a sentence with a proposition.

****

There was a young doctor named Beebee,
Wished to wed a nurse name of Phoebe.
    "But," he said, "I must see
    What the clerical fee
Be before Phoebe be Phoebe Beebee."

****

Nurse Mary Patton once remarked how odd it was that our parents, who knew little and cared less for child psychology, yet managed to raise superb Americans.

****

"Stay away from those square meals," Nurse Albers advised her patient. "In your case they tend to make you round."

TYPES OF NURSES: A FIELD GUIDE

As with flowers, nurses come in a variety of shapes, sizes, and colors. They come with all kinds of temperaments and personalities as well. In the hospital or other place of practice you have chosen, you will come to notice that the genus "nurse" divides itself into certain recognizable categories or species. Following are some of the stereotypical nurses you will encounter on your appointed rounds. Study them; get to know all their strengths and weaknesses. See if you can recognize the future you.

SWEET SUZIE, INNOCENT IDA, OR VIRGINAL VIRGINIA

The most angelic of the nursing species, these perpetually sweet R.N.'s retain the dewy-eyed wonder of a sophomore at her first prom. Their soulful gaze is that which most offers reserve for newborn puppies. Male patients respond by rolling over and wagging their tails--and falling madly in love with these often-ineffectual angels of mercy. Sweet Suzie is far from efficient, spending most of her time fetching vases or fruit juice--but patients feel compelled to get better simply to avoid breaking this poor nurse's heart. (However, said patients had better pray she's not on duty if they go into cardiac arrest.)

BATTLE-AX BERTHA

Reminiscent of the nurse in *One Flew Over the Cuckoo's Nest,* these R.N.'s mean business! Lights out means lights out--it doesn't matter if another nurse is taking blood at the time. These tough mamas didn't make it into the Marines, so they're revolting (are they ever!). Don't even think of crossing them, because they've got the rules on their side (often tattooed on their bulging biceps). Bertha can't for the life of her understand how anyone pulling a double shift could feel overworked. Need it be said that her favorite patients are Hell's Angels, pro wrestlers, and hit men? She dreams about serving hospital food to Rambo--and forcing him to eat it. Battle-ax Berthas are certain half of the patients shouldn't be "lazing around" in the hospital to begin with, and the positive function of these distaff dictators is intimidating patients into feeling healthy enough to check out.

LAZY LUCY

Call light on? She "didn't see it." She's not tired from long shifts and being overworked; she's tired from staying up all night thinking up excuses for goofing off. She'll "get around to it eventually," but starting her morning rounds at 11:55 is pushing it a bit. Lucy is completely aware of what has to be done, and equally sure that if she doesn't do it, someone else will...she hopes. True, Lazy Lucy is therapeutically beneficial to many patients, who learn to do for themselves out of desperation. She can usually be found using the phone for an "emergency at home," or engaging in her favorite hospital activities--chatting and gossiping. Steer clear of this one, or you'll find yourself making her rounds--while she sneaks off to the nurses' lounge to watch *General Hospital.*

MOTHER MOLLY

Molly is a bit older, and therefore a bit wiser than the average nurse. Loaded to the gills with anecdotes of her nursing past, she's sincere, steadfast, and thorough--possibly *too* thorough. With five blankets, three of them thermal, a heating pad, a woolen bathrobe, and a sleeping pill that began working fifteen minutes ago, it's reasonable to conclude that waking a patient to find out if he or she is too cold might be unnecessary. Molly just wants to make sure that patients eat and sleep well. She wants to be sure the residents, nurses, orderlies, elevator operators, and visitors eat and sleep well. If you're single, she'll matchmake. If you're tired, she'll find you a place to rest. If you're hungry, she'll bring you home-baked cookies. She reads *Good Housekeeping* and *Reader's Digest,* talks about her family and their ailments, crochets--and wakes patients up to take their sleeping pills.

SEXIE SADIE

White fishnet stockings, mini-skirted uniforms, and gallons of perfume are her trademarks. Because she goes braless, Sadie must *by all means* be kept away from the cardiac unit. She's *The Sensuous Nurse* in the flesh. In school, her only high grades were in biology, and even then she needed "special tutoring sessions" from the prof. Sadie gets consistently high temperature readings from her male patients, and they often develop high blood pressure--as do the doctors. She always knows where there's an empty bed--and she makes sure it doesn't stay empty for long. She loves to work the night shift and will often yell "STAT" when there's a cute resident on duty. Sexy Sadie's greatest nursing skills are bringing male patients out of comas, keeping elderly men in absolutely top form, with their reflexes sharp, and motivating female patients to get well quickly so their male visitors won't be tempted by Sadie again.

BITCHIN' BRENDA

No matter how overworked and exhausted you are, Brenda is more so. This little princess got everything she wanted, and she really thought nursing would be a breeze. Her diligence is far surpassed by her complaining--in fact, she bitches and moans enough for the entire shift, making her a true wonder in the morale department. If Brenda won the lottery, the first thing she'd do would be bitch about not finding a bank close by enough to deposit the money at. In Brenda's life, nothing is *ever* right. Her boyfriend's new Renault doesn't have enough leg room, and besides, it rained the whole first day of their Caribbean vacation. Brenda chose the wrong profession--and she is vociferous about this fact. She finds it depressing to be around sick people, and will often complain to ICU patients (those who are conscious, that is) about her ruined manicure. Her greatest asset to the patients is that after listening to her gripe and bitch, they not only don't feel so bad, but they start gathering the strength either to kill her or go home.

TATTLETALE TINA

Tina is extremely observant; no detail of hospital life, no matter how petty, escapes her eagle eye and sharp tongue. She's often the head nurse's pet, since she keeps the head nurse informed about potential blackmail situations and malpractice suits--as well as humane rule-bending on the part of her fellow staff members. Her eye for details, such as cigarettes butt brands, lipstick stains, and alcohol on the breath, would qualify her for a career as a private detective or medical examiner, but she prefers to be a petty, back-stabbing hospital snoop. Tattletale Tina might even make an excellent nurse, if only she would turn her eagle-eyed attentions to the patients under her care.

(From the *Unofficial Nurse's Handbook* by Richard Mintzer and Nina Schroeder. Copyright © 1986 by Ultra Communications Inc. Used by permission of New American Library, a division of Penguin Books USA Inc.)

WHINORRHEA:
NEW UNDERSTANDING OF AN OLD CONDITION
By Elizabeth A. Schultz, RN, BSN

Marsha took a deep cleansing breath before entering Room 519. It was only midnight and she had already answered Mrs. Gorski's call light four times. The evening nurse had given Mrs. G. a Halcion at 9:30 and assured Marsha that she would sleep through the night. Another empty promise.

"What took you so long?" Mrs. G whined. "I called 10 minutes ago. What if it had been an emergency? I could be dead by now ... maybe that would be a good thing. I wish I were dead."

"Mrs. Gorski," Marsha said calmly, "I saw your light go on from down the hall. I finished what I was doing and came directly to your room. I've been in here five times and I really do need to check my other patients before it gets much later. Now, what can I do for you?"

"Don't argue with me, young lady! I just told you that I wish I were dead and all you want to do is defend yourself and call me a liar. Some nurse you are!" Mrs. G cast her eyes to the ceiling and batted them furiously as if fighting back tears.

"You wish you were dead, Mrs. Gorski?" Marshal reflected, using her therapeutic communication skills.

"That's what I said, isn't it?" Mrs. G snapped.

"Would you like to tell me about it, Mrs. Gorski?"

"Well, I'm sure you don't really care, no one does, but I really need someone to listen to me for a change. All my life I just give, give, give to my family and friends and now, when I'm knocking at death's door, where are they? I'm living in pain and they just carry on as if nothing had changed. No one comes to see me. No one cares."

Again using therapeutic communication, Marsha attempted to explain Mrs. G's surgery, an appendectomy, and emphasized the fact that her condition was not at all critical. She had suffered no complications and would be discharged in a day or two. Marsha also pointed out that Mrs. G's husband visited every evening after work and her children stopped by or called every day as well. She asked Mrs. G what she thought about all the cards and flowers in her room.

"Guilt!" Mrs. G blurted. "Pure, unadulterated guilt. They're just going through the motions. I knew you wouldn't understand. And as for my condition, Miss Know-It-All, I know they're not telling me the truth. I'm sure I have cancer and that weasel I'm married to won't let them tell me."

Marshal acknowledged Mrs. G's obvious anxiety and encouraged her to discuss her fears with her doctor in the morning. Then Marsha offered to help her get settled for sleep.

"Sleep? I haven't slept in days. I can't get comfortable. These flowers give me a headache. My water is warm and tastes like plastic. This place is too noisy and those sleeping pills don't do a damn thing. I think they're giving me placebos. I'm sure you're dying to get out of here, so why don't you just run along. Your coffee's probably getting cold and you're missing out on all the juicy gossip at the nurses' station."

Marsha fluffed the pillows and straightened the covers. She placed her hand on Mrs. G's shoulder, looked into her eyes with her most compassionate gaze and said, "Good night, Mrs. Gorski. I hope you rest well." She wanted to take the call light away, but instead placed it well within Mrs. G's reach. "I'll be close by if you need me."

Does this sound familiar? Although Mrs. G's case may be a bit extreme, it is a classic example of an age-old condition that has only recently been named and understood physiologically. It is called whinorrhea and so far, two types have been identified: acute and chronic. Mrs. G obviously suffers from the latter. This is much more serious and as of yet, essentially untreatable. This article focuses on recognizing and preventing acute whinorrhea.

What is Whinorrhea?

In recent years, research pathologists have identified a gland, the whinalot, which is nestled between the intermediate and anterior

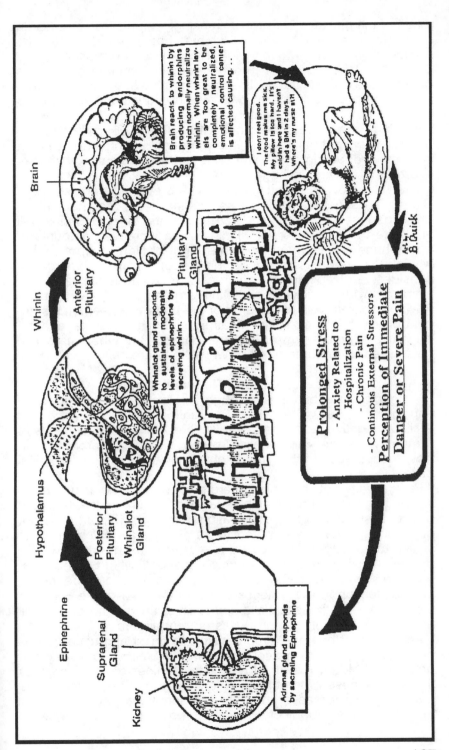

lobes of the pituitary. Through increasingly sophisticated research technology, a new hormone, whinin, has been detected. Its composition is similar to that of ACTH but was never differentiated until 1981, when Dr. I. M. Smart discovered minute differences between the two. He traced its secretion to the tiny whinalot gland, which was previously believed to be a nonfunctional appendix to the anterior lobe of the pituitary.

In adults, the whinalot averages .013 x .01 x .005 cm in size and 5-6 gm. in weight. It is considerably larger in infants and peaks in size and production of whinin during puberty, then slowly shrinks in size and activity until age 25.

The whinalot is sensitive to the secretion of epinephrine. Sensitivity is generally decreased in the adult, so that only a prolonged secretion of moderate amounts of epinephrine will stimulate the production of whinin. When increased amounts of epinephrine are secreted, as in the "fight or flight" response, the whinalot is suppressed. But as the perception of an emergency subsides, and epinephrine decreases to a moderate level, the whinalot instantly kicks in, secreting large amounts of whinin.

Whinin then travels to the area of the brain where emotions are controlled. It is most often neutralized by endorphins and no outward sign or symptoms are noted. But when it is not neutralized, symptoms of acute whinorrhea are seen.

Assessment of a Potential Whiner

Whinorrhea exhibits itself through incessant complaining in an annoying tone of voice, which frequently fluctuates in pitch and elicits a negative response in the listener, obliterating all traces of sympathy. It serves no beneficial purpose to the sufferer and can slow recuperation in the already physically compromised hospital patient.

Patients are not the only sufferers of whinorrhea. It has been known to strike members of the health care team; usually because of relentless stress or by association. Although whinorrhea is not contagious, it has been noted to be somewhat "catching." It is similar to the suggestive powers of a yawn. Dealing with a whiner causes stress, increasing the nurse's susceptibility to whinorrhea.

Chronic whinorrhea is easily identified and can be noted immediately upon the patient's arrival to the floor or the ER. As stated before, it is essentially untreatable, unless the doctor will allow administration of high doses of tranquilizers.

Acute whinorrhea has a more insidious onset and usually does not show up until the patient has been hospitalized for at least 24 hours. Early identification of a potential whiner greatly increases the effectiveness of treatment. A few steps can be added to the nurse's admission assessment to help identify a potential whiner before he goes into full-blown whinorrhea.

Ask the patient if he feels that he experiences more than his share of bad luck. If he answers yes, you can be 90% sure that you have a whiner on your hands. Negativity is a major contributing factor to whinorrhea.

Next, inflict a little pain and note the reaction. Sudden pain is known to cause instant and brief episodes of whinorrhea in those prone to the disease. Observe the patient while his blood is being drawn or while you are starting his IV. If necessary, step on his toe or drop your clipboard on his shins. The pain test is a good assessment tool...use it.

Lastly, talk to the patient's family, if possible. They can usually tell you if the patient is prone to whining.

Treatment

Once Dr. Smart identified the whinalot gland and its function, the controversy over whether to treat whinorrhea began. Biochemist Dr. I. B. Smarter immediately set to work on a cure. He developed Anti-Whinin Factor (AWF), which prevents secretion of whinin. The AMA was not easily convinced that this was a condition that required intervention. Since doctors spend an average of five minutes per day with hospitalized patients, whining did not affect them. Nor did they realize the effect of whinorrhea on healing.

In 1988, nursing researcher Ima Angel did a comprehensive

study of those effects. The following are a few of her conclusions: whiners take 150% longer to heal than non-whiners, use 100% to 200% more pain meds and are 5 times more likely to develop complications. These and other undisputed statistics spurred the AMA into approval. In November, 1989, the FDA approved the use of AWF in the hospital setting.

Daily administration of intravenous AWF is highly effective, but therapy must begin before the whinalot begins secretion of whinin. This is why early detection of potential whiners is crucial. Patients are given a loading dose of 1 gram, then 500 mg/day during the course of their hospital stay. AWF not only inhibits the secretion of whinin but also increases production of endorphins.

Although it is a relatively safe drug, AWF is not without side effects. One percent of patients who receive AWF develop "Pollyanna Syndrome" and become constantly cheerful, compliant and completely unassertive. Also monitor your patient for hypertension, apathy, nausea/vomiting, vertigo and inappropriate or incessant laughter.

Chronic whiners like Mrs. Gorski will always be around, but studies show that only 20% of all cases are chronic. This means we now have the capability of effectively treating 80% of our whining patients. As nurses we are taught to focus on the needs of the patient, but just think how much more pleasant our jobs will be once AWF gains widespread acceptance. If your hospital is not using AWF, suggest it. It can save you and your patients hours of whining.

(Reprinted with permission of Elizabeth A. Schultz, RN and art work by Bob Quick of Bob Quick Illustrations)

Help?*

When doctors doctor, and nurses nurse,
Most patients get better, though some get worse.
The system's not perfect, but one of the facts is
That no one is suing the nurse for malpractice;
She knows what her job is, and does it with grace,
While doctors make sure that she stays in her place.

Now nurses start doctoring; Junior Physicians?
Noctors? or Durses? Nurdocs? Nursicians?
What will their work be? And how shall we choose them?
How to be certain the public will use them?
And how to get doctors (traditional, staid)
To accept as their colleague this new Medi-Maid?

Perhaps aplenty, but what's even worse is:
If one of them's sued, they'll wish they were Nurses.

Michael M. Stewart, M.D.
Rockefeller Foundation

Bangkok, Thailand

*Reprinted with permission from the New England Journal of Medicine, ©1971;
285(24):1384.

****

"Well you wouldn't let us catheterize you."

Prostatic Resection,
Or Lines for My Urologist*

Now that at last, I lie so meekly here,
    My nether half benumbed, a prey to fear,
Good Doctor, I beseech you, have a care
    As you explore those tubes and ducts down there!
I hope that in your cystoscopic quest
    (As three diplomas on your wall attest)
With sponge, resectoscope, hawk-billed coudé
    You know just what you are about today!
Oh, do be careful as you probe and shove
    With catheter and sound and rectal glove,
While in my dank and murky depths you grope
    With tiny, incandescent telescope,
With practiced eye and craft superior
    To reconnoiter my interior.

I know you have, as yonder parchments state,
    The arcane skills that they certificate.
You dilate, snip, excise and cauterize;
    Such arts unfeignedly I eulogize
I do not doubt your virtuosity,
    But ponder, sir, what this can mean to me!
If you should falter--no offense!--I plead
    To what calamaties can all this lead?
What piercing pangs may we precipitate,
    What surging ecstasies abbreviate?
What dire impairments may your blade inflict,
    What cherished sins in future interdict?
As to the mark your nimble scalpel swoops,
    The word I do not wish to hear is "OOPS!"

Richard Bardolph
University of North Carolina
at Greensboro,NC

*Reprinted with permission from the New England Journal of Medicine, ©1980, 303(11):647.

"It's that Mrs. Kasher you said was in false labor.
She wants to know how to tie that false cord."

(Reprinted with permission of *Medical Economics*)

(*Sixth Over Sexteen*, J. M. Elgart, 1956)

5

PATIENTS

More men would look more spic if they didn't have so much span.

****

A 90-year-old woman was finally inveigled by her children to go to a psychiatrist. After the examination, the psychiatrist told the old lady that she had nothing to worry about, that she was in surprisingly good health for her age.

The old lady sniffed and slowly stood, then she pointed her finger at the physician and said, "Don't tell me I got nothing to worry about, young man. I was feeling lousy long before you were born."

****

There was a young fellow named Sidney,
Who drank till he ruined his kidneys.
        They shriveled and shrank,
        As he sat there and drank,
But he had lots of fun, didney?

****

The best medisin I kno for the rumatiz is to thank the Lord it ain't gout. *(Josh Billings)*

****

The patient in Room 228 is so fat that when she's out walking the halls, she looks like two puppy dogs fighting in a gunny sack.

****

"How's your uncle getting along since the operation?"

"Great. His busted leg is healed and he's usin' it as if nothin' had happened. You know the doctor said he'd have him walkin' within a month."

"Great. That he's walking again."

"Yep! The doctor sent him the bill and he had to sell his car to pay it. That's why he's walkin'."

A reporter was interviewing the town's oldest citizen, who had just celebrated his 100th birthday. "To what do you attribute your ripe old age, your longevity?" the reporter asked.

"Well, I never smoked, drank alcohol, overate or overindulged in anything. And I get up at six o'clock every morning."

"But I had an uncle who lived exactly like that and yet he lived only seventy years. How do you account for that?"

The old man considered the question for a few moments, then said, "He didn't keep it up long enough."

****

The girl in Room 536 is so skinny that if she turned sideways and stuck out her tongue, she'd look like a zipper.

****

The old man had had eight operations, almost one a year. But he was in good spirits when a friend came to call on him in the hospital. "How can you be so derned chipper, so cheerful after all those operations? Was this last one hard to take?"

"Not so bad," replied the patient. "I guess I'm getting used to it all. But I don't think I'll have any great problem in the future."

"What makes you so sure?"

"They put zippers on me this time."

****

That wonderful fictionist, Don Marquis, once said, "Eat, drink and be merry, for tomorrow ye diet."

****

Worry kills far more people than work. Perhaps that's why some folks do neither.

****

Johnny Leftsin had never done a lick of work in all his life. They took him to the doctor and had to get an explanation for Johnny's lack of get-up-and-go. The doctor examined Johnny and labeled his trouble as "Voluntary Inertia."

****

Folk wisdom has it that the fastest way to cure a baby of water on the knee is to hand it back to its mother.

"The remedy is simple," said the doctor to his patient. "I want you to drink a cup of hot water every morning."

"That'll be easy, Doctor. Why, I've been doing that for years. Only my wife calls it coffee."

****

Mark Twain once got a letter from a friend that complained of various ills the friend suffered. "Is there anything worse than having an earache and a toothache at the same time?" the friend wrote.

Mark Twain replied: "You bet there is! Count yourself lucky not to have rheumatism and Saint Vitus dance!"

****

"What a wonderful thing is youth," a lady remarked to the famous statesman, George Bernard Shaw.

Shaw replied, "Yes, and what a shame to waste it on children."

****

God heals, and the doctor takes the fee. *(Ben Franklin)*

****

The physician was giving the obese patient a thorough examination. When he started measuring his belly, he gave a low whistle and said, "Sir, you really must get rid of this useless basket you are hauling around on your middle. Your belly is enormous!"

"Aw, Doc, for a man my size it isn't so very big. I'm six feet tall, y'know."

"Maybe so," the doctor replied, "but you should consider your stomach in this light: If you were a tree, you'd be eighty-five feet tall!"

****

It is hard to believe but records tell us that a certain man heard that most accidents occur within twenty miles of home. So the quirky jerk moved to a town one hundred miles away.

****

If I was as bad as they say I am,
    And you were as good as you look,
I wonder which one would feel the worse,
    If each for the other was took.

| Doctor: | "And how is your husband feeling since I gave him that last medicine?" |
| Patient's Wife: | "Well, he's kinda better, sometimes, and sometimes he's worse! But from the way he carries on when he's better, Doctor, I really think he's better when he's worse." |

****

That very wise man, G. K. Chesterton, said that psychoanalysis is confession without absolution.

****

A man went to see his doctor to see if anything could be done to relieve his increasing baldness. "It's coming out like flags on the Fourth of July, Doc! Can you help me at least slow it down, if you can't grow it back?"

"I think so," his doctor replied. "Use this ingredient twice a day, patting it into your scalp, and don't wear a hat while you are using it."

"Good!" the man said happily. "But, Doc, are you quite sure it'll work?"

"Ya dern tootin' I'm sure. Y'see that examination table over there? Well, a month ago I spilled about a teaspoonful of this stuff on the table and now I have to shave it...every morning!"

****

"Doctor, was the operation a success? Will I be all right?"
"Sorry, old man, but I'm St. Peter."

****

The doctor told Mrs. Brown not to climb the stairs in her home until she had the cast removed from her broken leg. After several weeks she made a visit to the doctor and he told her that after the next weekly visit, he would remove the cast and she could, once again, climb the stairs in her home.

"Oh, thank goodness, Doctor. I'm so tired of shinnying up and down that drain pipe of mine."

****

When the bad news about smoking first appeared, a man offered his wife a thousand dollars to quit smoking. She did. Now he's offering her two thousand to stop talking about it.

178

First psychiatric patient:	"I'd be fine if I didn't have this endless hole in my head."
Second psychiatric patient:	"You're lucky. I got two holes in my head."
First patient:	"You and your holier-than-thou attitude."

****

When I woke this morning, I felt fit as a fiddle, really good. Then I walked to the bathroom, looked in the mirror and discovered that I looked more like a saxophone than a fiddle.

****

Did you hear about the girl who took the pill with a glass of stagnant pond water? She is now three months stagnant.

****

"I never denied that I'm a lazy feller," the small town bum said, "but my grandpa was a lot lazier. One time he got the seven-year itch and derned if he didn't get six months behind in his scratchin'."

****

Peoples' mouths are smaller than their brains, but the former seem to have much greater production than the latter.

****

In early England, they had a unique way to cure warts. You stole a dishcloth, rubbed the wart with it and then buried the dishcloth. *Viola!* The wart was gone.

Another way to rid oneself of a wart was to steal a bean, halve it, rub the halves on the wart and then heave them over your shoulder. As you heave them, you say, "Go, wart!" And the wart'll be gone.

****

It so happens that fat is one of those things that most Americans can accumulate!

And yet, another test to determine if one is overweight is to go into a phone booth. If you must back out to get out, you are too fat.

Some folks try desperately to lose weight and can't seem to get the job done. Medical annals show that one patient, despairing of the usual methods of weight reduction, all of which failed him, decided to go to an acupuncturist to see if he could get it to leak out!

****

There's a four-letter word that fatties hate: diet.

****

Operation to Make Me Sterile

The proliferation of birth control techniques in the modern world has not yet solved the problems of unwanted pregnancies. In the following text from Manchester, England, in 1978, a simpleton seeks professional help. Because of his and his wife's inability to understand the mechanics of diverse methods of contraception, he is forced to take a desperate measure.

Dear Sir,

I wish to apply for an operation to make me sterile. My reasons are numerous and after being married for seven years and having seven children, I have come to the conclusion that contraceptives are totally useless.

After getting married, I was told to use the Rhythm method. Despite trying the Tango and Samba my wife fell pregnant and I ruptured myself doing the Cha Cha Cha apart from which where do you get a band at five o'clock in the morning.

A doctor suggested we use the 'Safe Period.' At that time we were living with the in laws and we had to wait three weeks for a safe period when the house was empty. Needless to say this didn't work.

A lady with several years experience informed us that if we make love whilst breast-feeding we would be alright. It's hardly Newcastle Brown Ale, but I did finish up with clear skin, silky hair and wife pregnant.

Another old wives' tale was if my wife jumped up and down after intercourse this would prevent pregnancy. After constant breast feeding from my earlier attempt if my wife jumped up and down she would finish up with two black eyes and eventually knock herself unconscious.

I asked a chemist about the 'Sheath.' The chemist demonstrated how easy it was to use, so I bought a packet. My wife fell pregnant again which doesn't surprise me as I fail to see how Durex stretched over the thumb as the chemist showed me, can prevent babies.

The 'Dutch Cap' came next. We were very hopeful of this as it did not interfere with our sex life at all. It did give my wife severe headaches. We were given the largest size available but it was still too tight across her forehead.

Finally we tried the 'Pill.' At first it kept falling out. Then we realized we were doing it wrong. My wife then started putting it between her knees, thus preventing me from getting anywhere near her. This did work for a while until the night she forgot the pill. You must appreciate my problem.

Yours sincerely,
Dick Sinagen

(Reprinted from *Never Try To Teach A Pig To Sing*, by Alan Dundes and Carl R. Pagter by permission of the Wayne State University Press)

****

Its tough to be hard-of-hearing, but, somehow, such folks manage to make it. Just listen to this dialogue of two "kinder deef" guys.

"Can you tell me how to get to Adams Street?"
"What's that, stranger? I'm a leetle deaf."
"I beg your pardon?"
"I said I'm a leetle deaf."
"You don't say...I'm a little deaf, too."
"Too bad. Now what was it you wanted?"
"How to get to Adams Street."
"Oh. Sure. Just go down this here way for four blocks, then turn right. It's the third street down."
"That's Adams Street?"
"Oh, no. Excuse me, old feller. I thought you said Adams Street."
"Never heard of it. Sorry, stranger."

****

The Agriculture Department states that nearly 1,200 pounds of food is consumed annually by the average American. Naturally, a lot of it goes to *waist*.

Ode to the Circumcised Male

We have a new topic to heat up our passions--the foreskin is currently top of the fashions.

If you're the new son of a Berkeley professor, your genital skin will be greater, not lesser.

For if you've been circ'ed or are Moslem or Jewish, you're outside the mode; you are old-ish not new-ish.

You have broken the latest society rules; you may never get into the finest of schools.

Noncircumcised males are the "genital chic"--if your foreskin is gone, you are now up the creek.

It's a great work of art like the statue of Venus, if you're wearing a hat on the head of your penis.

When you gaze through a looking glass, don't think of Alice; don't rue that you suffered a rape of your phallus.

Just hope that one day you can say with a smile that your glans ain't passé; it will rise up in style.

(Reprinted with permission from Edgar J. Schoen, M.D., Oakland, CA)

****

Jake Thomas cured himself of worrying. "I finally convinced myself," he said, "that worrying is like a rocking chair...it gave me something to do but it didn't get me anywhere."

****

Grandma: "You know, I feel much better now. My stomach ache is almost gone. And wasn't it kind of the minister to come all the way over here to see about my pain?"

Daughter: "But, Mother, that wasn't the minister! That was the new doctor from town who came out here to see you!"

Grandma: "Well, what do you know! I did think he was a little familiar for a minister."

****

A certain doctor, overworked with patients during an epidemic, had this sign posted on his entrance door: "TO SAVE TIME, PLEASE BACK INTO THE OFFICE."

****

Laughter is like loosening a tight collar...it doesn't permanently solve any problems, but it makes things more acceptable for awhile.

It is interesting to see how our pioneers devised folk remedies for hurts and diseases for which they had no professional means of treatment. Here is a sampling from *Kiss A Mule, Cure A Cold* by Evelyn Jones Childers (Peachtree Publishers, Atlanta, GA, 1988).

Internal worms: Chew tobacco and swallow the juice.

Ringworm: Smear the juice of black walnut hulls on the hurt.

Warts: Tie small rocks equal to the number of warts in a cotton bag, then bury the bag. The warts will have gone when the bag will have rotted.

Crows' feet: This wrinkling that accompanies age can be eliminated by mixing five ounces of dried willow bark in a quart of water for six hours. Then boil and let simmer for fifteen minutes, strain and apply to the crows' feet wrinkles.

Nausea: Take a copper penny and place it on your naval.

Diarrhea: Certain foods will help. They are toasted bread, applesauce, rice, cinnamon, holly and papaya tea.

Acne: Rub pimples with toothpaste. Also helpful is the technique of using a freshly laundered diaper after it has been thoroughly impregnated with baby urine and placing it on the acne.

Abscess: Soak white bread in milk, then drain and place on the abscess.

Athlete's foot: Hot cow manure is best. Rub it on the rawness. If cow manure is not available, horse manure can be used, although it is not as effective.

Bags under the eyes: Place wet teabags on the swelling.

Migraine headache: Saturate a towel with vinegar, then wrap it around your head.

Skin cancer: Make a poultice of mandrake and periwinkle and lay it on the cancer. This will also remove warts effectively.

Ulcers: Take six ounces of milk, followed by two tablespoons of olive oil.

Improvement of the complexion: Wash your face in the first frost of the year.

To cure insect stings or bites, use the following: A wad of chewing tobacco, or a paste of wet snuff, or a slice of raw onion, or the juice of an aloe plant.

Poison oak:	Mix gunpowder with sweet corn and rub on the itching areas. Gunpowder can be procured from shotgun shells.
Swellings and bruises:	The leaf of the common weed, the mullein, should be picked, then dried, or used fresh, by placing on the swelling or bruise for quick recovery.
For early infection:	Place a green grapeleaf on the sore. Or use a pulp made from banana peels.
Sores:	Use a mixture of lard and sulfur on the sores.
Hiccups:	Fill a glass of water, then bend forward until you can drink out of the far side of the glass. Drink all the water. You can also try swallowing a sip of vinegar, breathe into a paper bag or eat a teaspoonful of salt.
Sty on the eye:	Place a gold object on the sty. A wedding ring, stickpin or like object will do.
Sore throat:	This affliction can be eased by placing a raw onion in an old sock and tying it around the neck. Some say the dirty old sock itself is enough to affect a cure.
Laryngitis:	Gargle with vinegar, rain water and salt, several times daily.
Cough:	The common redbud bark should be taken from the north side of the tree, then boiled in water and sweetened with honey. This makes an elegant and effective way to get rid of a cough.
How to avoid cold altogether:	Rub your body with bear grease! Or, catch an oak leaf before it hits the ground. It helps to hang pieces of peeled onions over each doorway of your home from October until the following May.
Rheumatism:	If you would avoid this painful disease, carry some buckshot in your pocket, or a buckeye. Copper wire, worn as a bracelet, will ward off rheumatism. Also effective: sleep with your workshoes under the head of your bed.
Hemorrhoids:	Steep pine needles in hot water and hold your butt over the emerging steam.
Toothache:	A splinter from a tree that has been struck by lightning, when used as a toothpick, will likely ease the pain.
Chest pains:	Chew foxglove for pain around the heart. Foxglove is the source of digitalis, and digitalis is a medicine often prescribed today for such symptoms.

To ward off the doctor: Eat an apple a day for a sure thing, as we all know. But equally effective is an onion a day.

Insomnia: Place some violets in your bedroom.

Side pain (when walking): Pick up a rock, spit under it and the pain should disappear.

(From *Kiss A Mule, Cure A Cold,* by Evelyn Jones Childers. Published by Peachtree Publishers, Atlanta, GA. Reprinted with permission of the publisher.)

****

There was a young lady named Perkins,
Who just simply doted on Gherkins.
    In spite of advice
    She ate so much spice,
That she pickled her internal workin's.

****

Advice iz like caster oil. Eazy enuff tu give but dreadful oneazy tu take. Josh Billings.

****

The manager of a National Grocery chain store once remarked: "Have you ever noticed the kind of people who shop at health food stores? Y'know they all look like comparison shoppers for Forest Lawn!"

****

That same manager tells of meeting an old friend he hadn't seen in twenty years. "How goes it with you, Buddy?" he greeted his old friend. "Not so good," was the reply. "I've got bad arteries, emphysema, ulcers, arthritis, high blood pressure and lots more." "That's awful," the other guy said, "what are you working at now?" "Same old job," the poor guy replies. "I'm still selling health food."

****

Their physician recommended an exercycle for Mrs. Jones and her husband, both too fat and too lethargic. So she bought him an exercycle, and for herself...a sidecar to go with it!

****

An apt phrase states it very well: he who indulges...bulges.

It is imperative that patients listen carefully, very carefully to what the doctor tells them. An example: A girl darned near ruined her health and her reputation because she was inattentive to what the doctor prescribed for her. She thought he prescribed three hearty males a day!

****

"You've got to take it easier, Mrs. Beedle. Stop driving your husband so hard."

(From the *Wall Street Journal*. Reprinted with permission of Cartoon Features Syndicate)

****

Dr. William Osler used to tell his patients this story: A doctor once told a foreign patient that each morning he should drink hot water, an hour before breakfast.

A week later the man came to the office and announced that if anything he felt even worse than before his last visit.

"Did you do as I told you...drink hot water an hour before breakfast each morning?" the doctor asked.

"I try! I try!" the patient said, "but I no could kip eet op more dan 15 minutes."

Every chair in Dr. Harold Olson's Chicago office was taken. And still patients kept coming into the office. Obviously, things were moving very slow-w-wly. Finally, an old man stood up and announced: "Looks to me like I'd be just as well off to go on home and die a natural death."

****

"Doctor, can you help us? My poor husband thinks he is a World War I pilot."
"I can try. I have an opening at three o'clock, Friday."
"But, Doctor, that's impossible! My husband must appear in court then, charged with flying too low over the county courthouse."

****

Enjoy life. This sure ain't a dress rehearsal.

****

Eddie Hassan Peffer was up in years and constantly in and out of the doctor's office. Each time he went, the doctor performed operations of one sort or another, in hospital and out; adenoids, appendix, a bit of his ulcerous stomach, on and on and still the poor guy felt bad.
At last, Mrs. Hassan Peffer had had enough. She absolutely rejected any further suggestions of needed surgery. "I'm just damned tired of other folks opening my male," she said.

****

URINALYSIS

Some bring their sample in a jar,
    Some bring it in a pot,
Some bring a sample hardly ample,
    While others bring a lot.

Some hide it in a paper bag,
    Some wrap it like a treasure,
Some quite undaunted, proudly flaunt it
    As if it gives them pleasure.

Some cork it up so tightly that
    It's quite a job to spring it,
Some let it slosh, almost awash,
    And some forget to bring it.

Syndrome-Reader's Scowl

To the Editor: I found a colleague of mine in a dark mood that I mistook for an ordinary depression. Upon consultation with a specialist I was horrified to learn that he suffered from syndrome-reader's scowl.

"Note the pained curl of the brow, the wandering, fearful eyes, the cowering posture," said the specialist.

"C'mon, Brandon," I said to my friend. "You just need to have a little fun. How about some exercise?"

"Not on your life," shouted Brandon. "I might get tennis elbow, runner's knee, or frisbee finger."

I had never known Brandon to refuse exercise. "Let's catch a movie then," I offered.

"No, no, no! Haven't you heard of popcorn-eater's grimace?"

"Intense, repetitive movements of the tongue and facial muscles in response to a morsel of popcorn lodged near the tonsils," explained the specialist. "Some victims have been known to insert a finger into the posterior pharynx and induce a gag reflex."

"Sounds beastly," I said. Brandon was agitated and weeping.

"Forget the movie," I said, trying to calm him. "We'll go to the opera instead."

"Never! If I enjoy it I'll get applauder's palms."

"Painful, erythematous swelling of the hands in response to a bravura performance," said the specialist.

Brandon limped away, complaining loudly that his orthotics needed adjustment.

"Your friend is very ill indeed," said the specialist, shaking his head.

"Is there nothing that will help him? What about psychotherapy?"

"He'll never submit to psychotherapy if he's heard about shrink-seer's sputter. It's an uncontrollable compulsion to speak openly about one's feelings."

The specialist was correct. We never heard from Brandon again. There were rumors that he had fled to the Bowery, where he has allowed a bad case of tipper's elbow to progress to doorway-sleeper's hip.

As for me, I sit before the pile of unopened journals on my desk, tapping my fingers, fearful of the next revelation. Finally, I can bear the pain no longer. I return to the specialist. He looks at my hands.

"Procrastinator's fingertips," he says sternly. "Be very careful."

(*Syndrome-Reader's Scowl,* by David Bateman; 1981; 305(26) 1595. Reprinted with permission of *The New England Journal of Medicine.*)

****

It's been said that love makes the world go around, and it does, but it's laughter that keeps us from getting dizzy.

A few old-timers will recall the famous medicine, Kidacol. It was guaranteed to keep you young...a veritable fountain of youth. In fact, a lady in her sixties who could neither read nor write took only half a bottle of Kidacol and then went on to teach a sixth grade class. But that's not all. There was an old man who took only one bottle of Kidacol after which, one morning, he was awakened by his wife and told to get up. "OK, if you insist," he told her. "But I ain't goin' to school."

In conclusion, let us offer final proof of the efficacy of this sterling remedy. A woman, just past ninety years of age, had taken Kidacol for less than one year and was taken to the hospital where she passed away. Too bad, but they saved the baby.

****

IT PAYS TO BE A GOOD STORYTELLER

An El Paso, Texas newspaper related the sad news of Dr. M. G., who lost a finger when a poisoned dog, to which he was giving an anecdote, bit him.

****

It's good to grow up and spread cheer...but not merely to spread.

****

There is much scholarly work now being offered about the value of humor in health. And the analysis of the relation between humor and health are complicated and profound. But one is put in mind of the American sage who wrote: "Humor can be dissected as a frog can, but the thing dies in the process and the innards are discouraging to any but the pure scientist."

****

Obesity: A surplus gone to waist.

****

Johnny Jenkins had a terrible cold but he mustered up the energy to place a long distance call. The operator responded and Johnny gave her the number.
The operator asked: "Sir, do you have an area code?"
Johnny replied: "It's just laryngitis, Ma'am."

189

MEDICAL COSTS

There's a side effect that goes with many of the new wonder drugs...it's called bankruptcy.

****

A young man and his wife, both blonde, were presented with a lovely boy with violent red hair. The husband queried his wife about this but she assured him that she had always been faithful. So the husband went to a geneticist and asked for a solution.

"Tell me, Sir," asked the geneticist, "how often do you have sex with your wife? Once a day?"

"No, Sir. Much less often than that."

"Once a month?"

"Nope. Less than that."

"Once every two months?"

"I'd say we have sex about twice a year...every six months, maybe."

"That's the answer," said the geneticist. "It's rust."

****

Just because people hit seventy is no reason for sex life to cease. Consider the case of the elderly couple who entered a physician's office to tell him that they weren't sure of their sexual relations...were they going about it in the right way. So they performed in the office, on the examination table, and the doctor assured them that they were doing everything exactly right. He only charged them a $10.00 fee, smiling when he said that he was quite pleased to be of such service to older folks.

During ensuing months, the old couple came back for additional visits because of their uncertainty as to their sexual technique. Finally the doctor asked them why they bothered to do this and the old man said, "Well, you see, Doctor, we're both married which means that we can't go to her house and she can't come to mine. Well, the cost of a hotel room is $125.00 so we come here for ten. And Medicare gives us back $8.00 of that."

****

Whoever said that women can't take a joke was sure wrong. Proof? Just look at some of their husbands.

****

Doc Burnett says that all a do-it-yourself man needs to make a bay window is a knife and fork.

"It all started when this guy said he could shrink
hemorrhoids without surgery..."

(Reprinted with permission of *Medical Economics*)

****

SURE SIGN

It's not by the lack of a fever you tell
That a patient is mending and soon will be well.
It's not by the fact that his tongue is uncoated,
His color is good, and his stomach's not bloated,
No, not by the fact that his pains now are less
That you know that he's starting to convalesce.
It's not that his pulse rate is steady and slow
And his blood pressure's down, now three days in a row...
Here's a sign of recovery, big as a bus:
He has given up praying, and started to cuss.

****

Two friends were discussing the charge for a medical visitation
at Dr. Piedmont's office. "He charged me twenty dollars for the first
visit and fifteen dollars for the second," the one man said.

So the other fellow goes to Dr. Piedmont's office about a
problem with his sinus. He greets the doctor in this way: "Doctor.
Here I am again!"

"To tell the truth," the doctor said to his patient in the hospital, "I had given you up. I figured there wasn't a chance of recovery. But your determination to live, your courage in not giving up, that is what saved you. I admire you."

"Thanks, Doctor. And please remember that when you make out my bill."

****

Humor is the puncture that lets the b--- s--- out of a stuffed shirt.

****

"I've been sleeping fine, Doctor, since I attended your lecture on insomnia."

"Great. And did you enjoy the lecture?"

"No, but, as I said, it cured my insomnia."

****

A major cause of ulcers, today, is that sufferers have climbed too many mountains that were molehills.

****

A man was admitted to the Illinois asylum for the disturbed and the officials soon discovered that he thought himself an artist, a painter. So they gave him easels, paints, brushes...everything he needed. After a month or so, he invited the staff to a one-man show of his work. When all officials were seated, the patient whisked the cover off his masterpiece and there before the assembled experts was a completely empty canvas. "Tell me, Doctors and Nurses, how do you like it?"

"It's great," one doctor offered, "but what is it?"

"It is a vision of the children of Israel crossing the Red Sea."

"Oh?" the doctor replied. "But where is the sea?"

"It's been driven back out of sight, as the Bible relates."

"Uh huh, I see. But where are the Israelites?"

"They've already got across the Sea."

"But tell us, where are the pursuing Egyptians?"

"They haven't got there yet!" said the patient.

****

A recent medical report has it that an alcoholic afflicted for more than fifty years died and was cremated. Rather, they tried to cremate him but he blew up and wrecked the joint.

Life seems to be God's joke on us. Our duty and mission is to figure out the punchline!

****

"Nurse, please, can I have a drink of water?"
"Of course. Thirsty, eh?"
"Nope. I just want to see how badly I leak from all those needles!"

****

Isn't it an amazing contradiction that guys will jog ten miles a day and then ride the elevator to the balcony?

****

Doctor: "Mr. Jenkins, I must be perfectly honest with you...very few patients have survived this operation that I feel you must have. Is there anything I can do for you before I begin?"
Patient: "Yep! Hand me my sox, shoes and pants!"

****

Just after God created Adam, the new man complained: "Oh, Lord, you have given the lion and tiger teeth and claws, the elephant terrifying tusks, the deer great running talent and the turtle a hard shell. You gave the birds wings to flee with, but me you have left without defenses. Why?"
"Never fear," said the Lord unto Adam, "I shall give you an indestructible and hidden weapon that will do you more good than any weapons of the lion, the elephant or the deer. I shall give you a power far beyond theirs, a power that will even save you from yourself."
"Please, Lord, oh please tell me what you give me."
"I shall give you a sense of humor," God replied.

****

Newspaper headline: INFANT MORALITY SHOWS DROP HERE

****

There's another advantage to being poor. Doctors will cure you faster.

193

The patient heard repeated knocks on the door of his hospital room. He yelled, "Come in!" A nurse entered, saying, "Please remove your gown and any other clothing." He complied. Finished with her work, the nurse then said, "You can hop back into bed now. Any questions?"

"Yes. Why did you bother to knock?"

****

Doctor: "How old are you, Mr. Jenkins?"
Patient (mournfully): "I'm eighty-two, Doctor."
Doctor: "Come, come, Sir, that's not so old."
Patient: "The heck it ain't. My grandkids came home from school yesterday and told me what they were studying in history. Why, Doc, those things were current events when I was in school."

****

Doctor: "Yes, Mrs. Edwards, I did prescribe a certain pill before each meal, followed by a small chaser of whiskey. Your husband is quite old now and he needs that which I prescribed. Is he taking it faithfully?"
Wife: "With the pills, he's a few days behind, Doctor. But he's three months ahead with the whiskey."

****

"And how is your husband sleeping, now, Mrs. Link? Is the sleeping powder working?"

"Oh, yes. It's doing better than I expected. You told me to give him a dose of powder that would fit on a nickel. But I didn't find a nickel so I used five pennies and he's sure been sleeping fine ever since."

****

The son had brought his grandmother to see Dr. Jong, a psychiatrist. "You see, Dr. Jong," the son explained, "She just isn't right up here (and he tapped his head). She's just too fond of waffles. That's all she talks about. It's an obsession with her."

"Well, now, that doesn't seem so disturbing," the physician responded. "I love waffles myself, eat them regularly, love them with maple syrup."

"Oh, really, Doctor?" the grandmother gushed. "How wonderful. You must come to my house this week. Why...I've got trunkload after trunkload just full of them."

Some said wisely, "Death is that condition that is merely nature's way of telling you to slow down."

****

You ask if he's overweight? Terribly! Real puffy. Last year he had the mumps for two weeks before he found out about it!

****

"George, you've been overweight for years. Why have you waited so long to come to me to see about it?"
"Well, Doctor, let me put it this way. Last Sunday at the golf course, I discovered that if I put the ball where I could hit it, I couldn't see it. And if I put the ball where I could see it, I couldn't hit it. That convinced me that it was time to come to your office!"

****

Doctor: "And how is your cold today?"
Patient: "Bad, Doctor. It's obstinate."
Doctor: "And how is your wife?"
Patient: "About the same."

****

Mrs. Jones brought her pregnant daughter to the doctor for the first visit. When asked the name of the husband, the mother replied, "All I know is that this baby is descended from a long line that my daughter listened to."

****

"Doc, that diet you gave me is sure hard to stay with. I'm doin' it but I'm so hungry I feel like my backbone is touchin' my belly button."

****

A woman entered a drugstore and asked for two dozen aspirin.
"Do you want them in a box, Ma'am?" the druggist asked.
"Oh, no! I'll just roll them home."

****

"That patient came in here looking terrible...all scratched up. In fact he looked like he'd been sortin' wildcats!"

"Now, Mrs. Blare, about the complications . . ."

You too can easily make a routine hysterectomy sound so risky that the patient gets hysterics. Just carry the doctrine of informed consent too far, as the M.D. does in this comical classic.

By William P. Irvin, M.D.
OBG specialist, Norfolk, Va.

After his lawyer left, Dr. Tom Jones sat at his desk, staring moodily out the window. He was thinking of what he'd just heard about informed consent. "I guess you have to warn patients about almost everything that might go wrong," he told himself. "I sure wouldn't like to get hit with a $100,000 verdict, like that radiologist who gave local X-ray treatments without telling the patient about possible burns.

His reverie was cut short by the entrance of his nurse. "Mrs. Blare is here, Doctor."

"Oh yes, she's to be admitted to the hospital tomorrow for surgery, isn't she? Send her in."

Mrs. Blare entered, sat down, and lit a cigarette. Then she said calmly: "Well, here I am, Doctor. My husband was a little upset until I told him you said it was just a fibroid tumor, just a simple hysterectomy, and there really wasn't much to it."

Dr. Jones winced. What his lawyer had told him made him sorry he'd used those words. "Now, Mrs. Blare, I didn't exactly mean it that way. You see..."

"Doctor, what is it? Do I have cancer?"

"No, still fibroids, Mrs. Blare. But a hysterectomy--well, frankly, there are some things that can go wrong. Not often, of course. But I think I should tell you of the possibilities."

"Oh, I'm not worried, Doctor. But if it'll make you feel better, go ahead and tell me."

"Well, after you're admitted to the hospital, they'll shave you. And occasionally they may nick the skin a little. ... No, I realize that's not so bad. ... Yes, I realize you're not the type to get upset over little things. ... Well, then they'll draw your water. Sometimes this can cause a little inflammation of the bladder. ... That's right--like you had with your last pregnancy. ... Well, I know it took four months, but usually we can cure it much faster. We'd use some of the newer drugs because they don't cause as many reactions. ... A reaction? Well, you break out in a rash and itch and... That's right--like your cousin, John, after he got penicillin. ... He died? Oh, I didn't know. Mrs. Blare, you're shaking ashes all over my rug.

"Next they'll draw some blood from your arm for tests. ... Yes, I know you've had it done before. But sometimes you can get a virus infection that causes a little liver reaction. ... Your friend's husband died too? Well, most people get better. Of course, it takes years sometimes, and--well, anyway, it doesn't happen often. Mrs. Blare, you look pale. Here, take this pill. That's better.

"Now at bedtime, they'll give you some drugs to help you rest. ... Yes, I guess you could get a drug reaction from them, but usually. ... No, I don't mean that would be your second drug reaction. I mean, you probably wouldn't have any reaction. ... Yes, I know what I said about the bladder.

"You'll also get a little enema at bedtime. ... Mrs. Blare, what happened to your cousin in Omaha has nothing to do with this case. They won't punch a hole in your intestine. ... Of course, I don't guarantee it. ... Peritonitis? Well, yes, a hole in the intestine can cause it, but nobody will punch a hole in your intestine. ... No, I was not aware that your brother is a lawyer.

"Well, let's see. Early the next day they'll take you to the operating room, which brings us to the anesthetic. Occasionally, it can cause a little problem. ... Well, the heart might stop working. ... Oh, yes, we can start it again. Usually. If we can get it going, it usually keeps on working O.K. Of course, if the brain has been damaged, the patient might not be too bright after surgery. ... Yes, an idiot, you might say--but really, that doesn't happen often.

"Next we open the abdomen and remove the uterus. Of course, once in a while--not very often, you understand--but just sometimes. ... Mrs. Blare, just because your grandmother said you were born under an unlucky star. ... Now stop shaking. Here, take another pill. ... No, it won't cause a drug reaction--I don't think. You mustn't worry so, Mrs. Blare.

"Now, in removing the uterus, we might--on very rare occasions, you understand--get into the bowel. ... I mean we might cut a small hole in the bowel. Sort of like the enema thing, yes. ... Well, we just sew it up. ... Yes, peritonitis is possible.

"If all goes well, and we haven't nicked the ureter. ... Oh, the tube that goes to the bladder. ... Well, it might cause a fistula and -- let's talk about that later. ... Yes, your insurance would cover it if it should happen.

"Now the uterus is out, and the incision is closed. ... No, we won't sew the bowel up too tight. I mean, we won't touch the bowel. ... Yes, I know what I said before. ... No, I'm not contradicting myself. Now, now, please relax. ... After the surgery you'll be given some fluids through a needle in your vein. ... Well, yes, I guess so. That old virus and the liver again. ... Yes, you mentioned that he died.

"If the wound doesn't break open we'll. ... Well, all your intestines would spill out. ... Oh, we'd put them back. ... No, that wouldn't cause idiocy.

"There's only one more thing. Of course, it doesn't happen often. We call it a Staph infection. ... Oh, you've read about it in the papers? ... They all died? But that was in a nursery. ... Well, yes, grownups can die from it, but we have drugs and. ... Well, a drug reaction isn't usually as bad as a Staph infection.

"To sum it all up, Mrs. Blare, a hysterectomy really isn't so simple. Now if you'll just sign this paper that says I've informed you of these little complica-- Mrs. Blare! We're not through! Where are you going? *Come back, Mrs. Blare!*"

****

Putting on additional weight in summer picnic days is something that really "snacks" up on people.

****

The perfume worn by Jane or Nancy,
Does more than merely stir the fancy,
Does more, indeed, with its aroma,
Than leave men in a helpless coma.

Bacteria and fungi squirm
No longer on the epiderm
That's daubed or sprayed or doused quite well
With scents of Lanvin or Chanel.

So tell the somewhat worried male;
Go on and sniff the girl, inhale;
You'll get the thrill that you'd expected,
And, what is more, be disinfected.

(*The Medical Muse* by Richard Armour, 1963. McGraw-Hill Book Co., New York, NY. Reprinted with permission of Mrs. Kathleen S. Armour, Claremont, CA)

A flim-flam artist posed as a doctor, set up an office with waiting room, examination rooms, nurses, receptionist and the like. He examined his first patient, an elderly lady, and suggested that she start on a regime of youth elixir that he guaranteed to work. "Only $150 a bottle," he told his patient. "It is guaranteed to give you 300 years of life," he told her, "or your money back." She bought one bottle, forked over the money and left, stopping at the receptionist's desk to ask, "Will this really let me live to be 300 years old?"

"I really can't tell you" the receptionist replied. "I've only been here 143 years."

****

A man applied for life insurance and, when asked the cause and age at death of his father and mother, he told the truth. "My mother died at age 36 of cancer. My father died at age 40 of tuberculosis." The agent said, "No dice," and tore up the application.

The man applied to yet another insurance company, but this time he played it more carefully. When asked what his father died from, he replied, "He was hit in the head by a pitched ball while playing baseball at age 96."

"And your mother? Her cause of death?"

"She was 92. She died. But they saved the baby."

****

There was a young man of Concises
Whose ears were of different sizes,
    The one that was small,
    Was no use at all,
But the other won several prizes.

****

Doctor: "Mrs. Egers, what is the most you ever weighed?"
Patient: "263 pounds.
Doctor: "And the least?"
Patient: "Seven pounds, three ounces."

****

Have you noticed how fat people seem to be good-natured? The reason is that it takes such a long time for them to get mad clear through!

The mother of triplets was visited by an old friend. As the triplets were brought out for admiration, the mother gushed: "It is positively unbelievable that I have triplets. Why do you know, Grace, they say it happens only once in 212,468 times."

"Well, I'll be darned!" her friend replied. "However do you manage to do your housework!"

****

Still More Over Sexteen, J.M. Elgart, Editor. 1954

****

Hospital patients, altogether bored and not able to find a deck of cards, swiped the diagnoses out of a nurse's pocket as she passed by. A game of draw poker was started and they bid high and over-raised each other until a huge pot of money decorated the table.

"Well, looks like I win," said one patient as he reached for the money. "I've got three gallstones and two appendixes."

"Hold on there!" yelled another, "I got four enemas."

"Dammit!" said the first. "You win the pot."

The reason many people get lost in thought is that it's such unfamiliar territory.

****

"How did you get yourself in this fix?" the physician asked his young patient, who was with child.

"Well, I made the wrong statement, I guess," she replied. "My boyfriend asked me if I'd mind if he stole a kiss and I said to him, 'What would you say to a guy who had a clear chance to steal a trunkful of money and only took a dollar bill!'"

****

The above story reminds us of the college poem:

"Explain sex," she said,
On the couch with me.
I figured I could 'cause,
She was past twenty-three.
"My darling," I said,
"I'll sure do as you bid,
But you'll have to bear with me."
And, by golly, she did!

****

The unclaimed treasure (an old maid) came to the psychiatrist and expressed herself in this way:

I've never been dated,
I ain't even been kissed.
They said if I waited,
No man could resist
The lure of a pure and innocent miss.
The trouble is this --
I'm sixtyish!

****

Doc, you say my operation was a success. I sure do thank you. Why, I'm as tickled as a dog waggin' two tails.

****

They say you can call yourself a senior citizen when most of the names in that little black book are doctors.

"Doctor, they tell me that the water in Chatham is unsafe to drink. What should I do to make it safe?"

"Glad you stopped by. The water really is unsafe. Here's what you do. First you filter it, then you boil it and then you add the right amount of chlorine to it."

"Will that do it?"

"Yes, if you drink beer only."

****

There was a young lady of Spain,
Who vomited while in a train,
    Not once, but again,
    And again and again,
And again and again and again!

****

Loss of memory can be a mighty distressing ailment, but sometimes it's funny.

"Where's the car?" demanded the absent-minded professor's wife.

"Dear me!" he replied, "Did I have the car today?"

"You certainly did. You drove it to your class."

"Now that *is* strange. I recall that after I got out of the car, I turned around to thank the student who had given me a lift and wondered where he had gone!"

****

To be careful with a dollar is, in many cases, a good trait. But some guys carry it a bit too far. Consider how these fellows followed doctor's orders, illustrated by two very tall tales...whoppers!

Self-help with sickness may be all right in some cases but not in all. Consider the case of the wife with troubled breathing. Her physician urged her husband to take her to the seashore for relief. But the guy was such a cheap SOB that he bought a herring, sat his wife in a chair and fanned her night and day!

And that is not the only recorded case of a chintzy husband!

A similar patient was requested to take his wife to the mountains for relief of her asthma. He bought a lovely picture of Aspen, Colorado, in winter, and fanned her daily with it!

"Doctor, you've got to help me...it's my husband," the woman groaned. "He thinks he's a refrigerator! Honest."

"Why, that's appalling. Tell me about it."

"Well, as I said, he thinks he's a refrigerator. And that keeps me awake. I haven't had a decent night's sleep in three weeks."

"I don't understand," the doctor said. "How does this refrigerator delusion of your husband keep you awake?"

"Well, you see, he sleeps with his mouth open and the light is so bright I can't sleep."

****

The parents were confused when their little girl asked where she came from So they took her to the family doctor and asked him to explain it to her. This he did.

"Does that satisfy you, Dear?" the parents asked, afterward.

"Not really. Sara comes from Detroit and I wondered where I came from."

****

Sometimes medical patients are inscrutable: their ignorance impenetrable; their relatives impossible and their pocketbooks...unopenable!

****

"George! You look terrible. Been sick?"

"Yep! Had walking pneumonia. And my derned doctor charged me by the mile."

"I had a doctor like that once. He told me I had low blood pressure. But when he gave me the bill, well, that cured it!"

****

One good thing about health food restaurants is that they add nothing to the food. But fifty percent to the prices!

****

Taking the birth control pill is a "no-win" proposition. If you take it you have side effects. If you don't take it, you have front effects.

****

We still have a few doctors who aren't what they're quacked up to be.

The young man had been having strange illusions about objects around him, objects that only he could see. The worried parents took him to a psychiatrist who talked a bit to the boy and then came to the conclusion that to really determine what was behind these hallucinations, he would give him a series of inkblots to identify. The lad saw a sexual image in each one shown him. After a couple of dozen showings, the doctor took the boy to his parents and said, "This lad is completely obsessed with sex. He saw something sexual in every image I showed him."

"I'm obsessed with sex!" the young man screamed, "You say I'm obsessed. Hah! And just who in hell has been showing me all those dirty pictures?"

****

"Doctor, I've got a silver dollar lodged between my teeth and jaw. Happened about a month ago."

"Why did you wait so long to come see me about it?"

"I didn't need the money until now."

****

There was once a patient who was frightened when the physician told him that smoking would shorten his days. So he quit...quit stone cold. Now his days seem a hundred hours long.

****

"Well, well, Mrs. Edgars...I've got really good news for you."

"Pardon me, Doctor, but I'm Miss Capper."

"Then let me reverse the words, Miss Capper. I'm afraid I've got bad news for you!"

****

A ninety-year old woman was expected never to leave the hospital so that when she asked her doctor if she might fulfill one lie-long ambition, to "do a streak," he sympathized with her wishes and told the hospital to allow it. She jumped out of bed, stripped off her gown and began to walk, then run down the hall, past several wards and out the reception room and through the lobby, then out the doors to the lawn where she ran past two old gentlemen patients who were deeply uninterested. But one did look up as she went past, turned to his friend and said, "Say, Joe, did you see that old girl run past. Do you know her?"

"I think it's an old friend who I ain't seen in years. She never was neat. Even now it looks like that dress she was wearing needs pressing."

"That Doctor Jones sure made a mistake in his diagnosis and the cure for Mary's weakness."

"Why what happened?"

"Well," he said. "Mary had been inside too long, doing housework and all. He demanded that George take her out in the sunshine, every day, and you know that was impossible. Just couldn't be done. But George is a swell painter, sells his paintings real good, too. So he painted a picture of the sun on the ceiling of their bedroom and put Mary under it, resting prone on the bed."

"What a good idea! Did she feel better after that?"

"Heck no! She got so derned sunburned, she had to be hospitalized."

****

"OKAY, NOW — WHAT SEEMS TO BE THE PROBLEM?"

****

There's a fitness club in Chicago where this sign hangs over the door to the ladies' room:

GIRLS WHO EAT A LOT OF SWEETS
ARE BOUND TO DEVELOP LARGER SEATS.

Methanosis

To the Editor: Dr. W. C. Duane freely admits in the paper he co-authored with Dr. M. D. Leavitt, "Floating Stools--Flatus versus Fat" (N Engl J Med 286:973, 1972) that his consistently floating stools were fortuitously noted to be associated with "a CH_4 excretion rate of near record proportion." This forthright admission of a high methane rating from one of our professional colleagues inspired the following limerick:

> Our thanks to frank Doctor Duane
> Who takes the time to explain
> Just how he had noted
> That his stools often floated
> Before they were flushed down the drain.

> He must have thought first, "Mama mia!
> Do I suffer from steatorrhea?
> But it cannot be that--
> There is no trace of fat."
> Which led to another idea.

> Well aware of the gas he unloosed
> The doctor quite shrewdly deduced,
> (Almost clairvoyant)
> His feces were buoyant
> Because of the methane produced.

(*Methanosis* by Milton J. Chatten, M.D. 1972;287(2):362. Reprinted with permission from *The New England Journal of Medicine*.)

****

Richard Monckton Milnes, a Victorian politician, uttered this deathbed quip: "My exit is the result of too many entrees!"

****

An old lady was sitting in the examination room when approached by a nurse who asked, "Ma'am, are you waiting for a Pap smear?"
"No, it's a tad too early for that. But I could drink a Seven-Up."

****

After the severe automobile accident, the patient confessed to the doctor that he knew he wasn't dead because he was hungry and his hands were cold.
"And what's that supposed to tell you?" the doctor asked.
"Well, if I'd died and gone to heaven I wouldn't have been hungry...and if my hands hadn't been cold, I'd be elsewhere!"

A new patient came to the office of the town's leading psychiatrist. When he was on the couch and sufficiently relaxed, the doctor said, "This is your first visit, Sir. Would you mind telling me about yourself from the beginning?"

"Not at all," responded the patient. "In the beginning I created Heaven and Earth..."

****

Did you hear about the screwy gent who stipulated in his will that he wanted to be buried in a "No Smoking" section of the cemetery?

****

One of these strange kind of goofy patients entered the office of Dr. Stuart Yaffee and sat down ver-r-ry carefully. The doctor began to question him. "What kind of work do you do?"

"I work in a traveling carnival, Doctor Yaffee. I stick my head through a canvas wall and people pay to throw baseballs at me. And do you know, Doctor Yaffee, I haven't been able to sit down for two weeks."

"What the dickens has sitting down got to do with people throwing baseballs at your head?" asked the doctor.

"I forgot to tell you...the owner also uses the back of me for a dart game."

****

Blessed is the man who can laugh at himself because it's a cinch he'll never stop being amused.

****

The examining doctor was checking the draftee to see if he was fit to serve.

"Were you in World War II?" he asked.
"Too young."
"Were you in the Korean War?"
"Too old."
"Were you in the Vietnam War?"
"Too scared."

****

Doctor: "Mr. Jones, the check you gave me came back."
Mr. Jones: "So did my earache."

Some Essential (?) Medical Terms

Aluym: A notebook where you paste up memorable photographs.

Aseptic: A fellow who, in spite of the best possible proofs, continues to doubt.

Anesthesia: The name of the daughter of the last Czar of Russia.

Chill: The cute name of the girl who fell down the hill following the boy who'd gone up to fetch a pail of water.

Compress: A vital instrument that sailors use to find their way around the ocean.

Fracture: A part of a whole, like 1/2.

Gash: Money in the form of gold, copper and silver.

Ligature: Better kinds of writing, such as novels or dramas of high artistic quality.

Menthol: That which pertains to the mind.

Nurse: A concentration of sounds, generally unpleasant. Bedlam.

Relapse: To ease the mind and body of strain by just sitting back or lying down and filling the mind with lovely thoughts.

Rupture: Ecstasy, what one feels upon seeing great art...or beautiful women.

Shock: An ocean fish with long sharp teeth that can tear a person to pieces.

Wound: A slang contraction of *will not*.

****

The old man walked into the doctor's office, hemmed and hawed a bit, then got down to business. "It ain't easy to talk about, Doc, but, y'see, well, ahem...it's just that I can't hardly make love to my wife no more. Ain't got no pep in them middle regions."

"Well, don't worry about that," the doctor said. "You aren't so young any more, y'know. Just how old are you, Sir?"

"Well, lessee now. My wife, she's eighty-three and she's a year older'n me so that makes me somethin' like eighty-two, don't it?"

"Age does lessen sexual drive, Sir. But when did you first notice the problem?"

"Well, first time it happened was last night. Now that wasn't too doggone bad. But I'll be dognabbed if it didn't happen again this mornin'."

****

A good wife and good health are a man's best wealth.
Of all home remedies, a good wife is the best.

There was a time when "the three r's" meant a romantic, poetic combination. Now it stands as follows: At 19, it's romance. At 39, it's rent; and at 69, it's rheumatism.

****

Doctor: "At present, do you take any form of exercise?"
Patient: "Sure do. Why, Doctor, last week I was out seven nights running."

****

A guy named Epperson had been in the hospital a long time. One night, the phone rang at the night nurse's desk and she took the call, inquired who was speaking and the guy said, "I'm Mr. Epperson's best friend. I just called to see how he's doing."
"He's doing just fine," the nurse replied. "He's due to be discharged in two days."
"Sure do thank you, Ma'am," the voice said.
"But who shall I say has called?"
"This is Epperson. Nobody tells me a damned thing around here."

****

To say, "big bust" is
    common
And hearing it, I'm not
    thrilled:
But I never knew what
    "big bust" meant
Until I had that prescription
    filled!

****

A questionnaire was sent to all the physicians in Pennsylvania concerning their favorite popular songs. The following four were the most popular as judged from the results of the questionnaire:

1. Liver, Stay 'Way From My Door.
2. Yes, Sir, Asthma Baby.
3. You Take The Thyroid And I'll Take The Low Road.
4. On A Bifocal Built For Two.

" GET RID OF THE HORSE AND EAT THE
OATS. "

****

The psychiatrist wanted to get away to play golf. But three women patients were in the waiting room and he decided to get it over with quickly. He walked into the room, pointed his finger at one woman and said, "Madam, you eat too much. That's your trouble. I've told you repeatedly to eat less. Eat less. But you don't. By the way, what's your cute little girl's name?"

"Candy," she replied.

"Ah, ha. You see? Your subconscious yearning for food led you to name your child as a food."

He turned to the second woman. "And I've told you often, often, to drop that grasping, acquisitive tendency of yours. Your miserly qualities, your constant hoarding is simply obvious. But tell me, what's your cute little daughter's name?"

"Penny," she replied.

"Ah, ha," roared the psychiatrist. "See how your subconscious dictates your life? Pennies, nickels, more pennies. Always thinking of money even when you name your child."

He looked toward the third woman but she was walking toward the door. She held tightly her little son's hand, saying, "Let's get out of here, Peter."

There is a terrifically overweight man in St. Paul, Minnesota, who got that way because he was something of a prude. He detested four-letter words, especially the one known as *diet*.

****

An overworked priest found himself getting confused and so mixed-up that he consulted a psychiatrist, who advised him to forget his religious duties for a bit, change into civilian clothes and go to New York for a day's rest. And the priest took the medical advice.

In New York, now in civvies, shirt and tie...all dressed up, he takes in a musical comedy, a few movies, visits museums and does all the sights. Too, he visits a bar and has a few drinks. A waitress comes to his table and asks, "Father, can I help you with something?"

"Now how did you know I was a priest?" he asks.

"Easy. I'm Sister Theresa and I go to the same psychiatrist."

****

The mother of nine children was expecting her tenth. So she thought it time to call all nine kids into the living room and announce the arrival of their sibling. "Children, I want to tell you that the stork will be coming to pay us a visit."

"Visit!" yelled the husband. "Don't say 'visit' around here. That stork *lives* here!"

****

Some stories just go on from one generation to the next. The following lovely tale is one of those never-die stories:

Little Jimmy walks into his Grandma's room and asks, "Grandma, where did mother come from?"

"The stork brought your mother, dear."

Then Jimmy walks into his father's room. "Dad, where did Grandma come from?"

"I thought you knew," Dad said. "She came by the stork."

"Well where did I come from, Dad?"

"The stork brought you, too, dear boy."

So the lad walked out of the house and over to the neighbor to see his buddy, Pete. "Pete," he said, "I've just found out an amazing fact. There have been no natural births in our family for three generations."

****

Have you noticed how fat folks seem to be living beyond their seams?

Cowboy medicine sometimes took very bizarre forms. The following example comes from Lewis Nordyke's *Cattle Empire: The Fabulous Story of the 9,000,000 Acre XIT* (New York: William Morrow & Company, Inc., 1949), pp. 140-41.

A healthy sense of humor was often the best solution to many western range problems. While on roundup once, the foreman of an outfit found that his crew was blessed with a chronic grumbler. This particular waddie never liked the camping place the cook had chosen nor the food he fixed and was constantly complaining about one thing or another. Wanting to keep harmony, the foreman took this in silence for some time, but finally he could stand it no longer. One day the cowboy came to him with a complaint about the food, and the foreman told him that there was nothing wrong with the food, that what he needed was some "liver-regulator." He suggested that the cook might be able to supply him with some of the medicine, which was kept in the grub box. Others of the crew took up the suggestion and urged the cowboy to try some of the cook's remedy.

Finally, after complaining his way through a meal, the grumbler walked up to the cookie and said, "Say, how about some of that liver-regulator they been tellin' me about? I hope it's better than the meals we been gettin'."

The cook looked him over.

"It sure is," he agreed and reached into the grub box. His hand came out with a cocked .45 in it.

"This is the best liver regulator I know about," the cookie said. "An' if I hear one more word outa you, I'm going to let you have a big dose of it."

The improvement in the waddie's health was remarkable.

****

Here is yet another example of early cowboy medicine. Those old boys knew a thing or three about the mechanics of "healing." From *The Humor of the American Cowboy*, by Stan Hoig, 1970. Reprinted with permission of the University of Nebraska Press. This episode or case is from Bill Jones of Paradise Valley, Oklahoma; *His Life and Adventures for Over Forty Years in the Great Southwest.* Donahue & Co., Chicago, 1914.

On another occasion there was a big, overgrown cow poke named Tall Cotton, whose specialty was going to sleep during duty hours, leaving the rest of the crew to do his share of the work. The boys took it for a time, but they finally decided that something had to be done about the matter.

Then came the day they found Cotton curled up in a haystack, boots off, sound asleep. The opportunity was golden. The boys rounded up a huge tarantula, killed it, and laid it close to Cotton's leg. Then they tied a pin on the end of a stick and jabbed the sleeping waddie a couple of times. Cotton came awake like a wild Comanche doing the snake dance and, at the same time, a cowboy rushed up and smashed the tarantula with his boot heel.

Cotton took one look at the dead tarantula and turned white. He began to get sick, even though the other waddies did their best to console him with stories of the horrible deaths they had seen as a result of tarantula bites. Finally, one of the crew, who laid claim to having read *Ten Thousand Things Worth Knowing,* as well as *Dr. Chase's Recipe Book*, offered to try to save Cotton, even though he admitted it seemed hopeless.

First the cowboy poured a pint of bear's oil down Cotton. When that started some of the poison coming out of him, they followed it up with a glass of soda, a cup of vinegar, and finally a quart of water in which a plug of tobacco had been soaking. For a while it seemed almost certain that Cotton was going to die from that tarantula bite; but the medicine was potent and, eventually, he was saved. After that, the crew had very little trouble with him lying down on the job, especially in haystacks.

****

Talk about puns! There was this lady who accidentally got some vinegar in her ear, of all places. Now she suffers from pickled hearing.

****

They tell the story of London during the bombing terror of World War II. Two Cockney ladies were working in the American military hospital when bombs fell perilously close.

"Sure an' they are terrible fierce. Liable to blow yer into maternity," said the one Cockney lady.

"Shure and y're right," said the other Cockney. "And yer wouldn't know who ter blame either."

****

A physician was making his daily rounds at the local hospital. "Nurse," he said, "on what day does this patient expect her baby?" "June fifth," was the reply. "And the next patient here?" "June fifth." "And this one?" "June fifth." The doctor was flabbergasted. "Now that's odd," he said. "Don't tell me this lady, too, is expecting her baby to arrive on June fifth." "That I don't know, Doctor," the nurse confessed. "She wasn't at the picnic."

Then there was the querulous patient about to undergo surgery. To the last, he was undecided. "Are you sure, Doc, that I got to have this operation?"

"For sure. Definitely."

"And nothing else would help? Osteopath? Medicine?"

"Sir, if you want to live, you must have this operation."

"OK. But then I must have a preacher."

"What? Why? Are you really that depressed?"

"Ain't depressed. Ain't even nervous. But if I got to be opened, I want to opened with prayer."

****

Diglossia: The odd situation where you think you have two tongues. Women love the "disability" because they can talk twice as much. Hypocrites like it if they come forked and with two faces!

****

They say that Groucho Marx so enjoyed the Mayo Clinic that he put on a white coat and went around acting like a physician. He stopped at one bed and took the lady's pulse, then said, "Madam, you have mice!"

****

A visitor to a huge drug manufacturing company was greatly impressed with what she saw. "Why," she said, "they've got drugs so derned new that they haven't discovered diseases for them yet."

****

There's a story about an old man who had waited two hours to see the doctor. Finally he stood up and said, "I think I'll go home and die a natural death."

****

"At my age," said the old lady, "every doctor says the same thing. It's either something I have to live with...or something I have to live without."

****

There is so much publicity on breast surgery and implants these days, that a song about such things has been written and published. The title is "THANKS FOR THE MAMMARIES."

Then there was the case of the professional upholsterer who had grown totally bald, the result of an illness. But things are looking up for him. He's growing *mohair* now.

****

Bertha came running into the house weeping wildly. "What's wrong, Dear. Tell me what's wrong?" her husband cried.

"Oh dear...I've been to the doctor's office and he told me that, as a result of my fall, I've got a flucky."

"A flucky? What the hell's that. I'll call him." So he goes to the phone, calls the doctor, says, "I see," and "Oh, yes," and "Thanks, Doc."

He turns to his wife. "Dear, you misunderstood him. He said, 'You got off...lucky.' He did not say: You got a flucky, but 'off lucky'."

****

Physicians can't do much to help a man who sows wild oats six days a week except to counsel him to go to church on Sundays and pray for a crop failure.

****

A young woman walked up to the admittance desk at the hospital. "I need to see an uptern," she said.

"I suspect that you mean intern?" the nurse asked.

"Whatever. I came for a contamination."

"Contamination? I think you mean examination, right?"

"Whatever. I guess I'd best go to the fraternity ward, right?"

"I suppose you meant to say maternity ward?"

"Uptern, intern ...examination, contamination, fraternity, maternity...what the hell difference does it make? I mean to tell you, Sis, that I ain't demonstrated in two months and I think I'm stagnant."

****

"Mr. Kaufman, it was a mighty close call," said the surgeon. "We almost lost you midway through the operation. Thank heaven for your strong constitution. It pulled you through remarkably, given your age and all.

"Mighty grateful to you," the patient said. "But do, if you please, remember what you just said when you make out the bill!""

The doctor completed his examination and then said to the patient, "Well, Madam, I think I know your problem, the cause of those cramps. But I'll need to verify my diagnosis by x-ray. Have you ever been x-rayed?"

"No, I don't think so. But I've been ultra-violated a few times."

****

"Old Doc Mason told me that if I want to retain my health, I got to cut out every blamed thing I enjoy," the old man complained to his buddy. "So I told him how much I enjoyed paying his bills."

****

Get-well cards are so funny these days that if you don't get sick you're missing a world of fun.

****

"DO ME A FAVOR, DOCTOR, AND STOP HUMMING 'I'LL BE SEEING YOU IN ALL THE FAMILIAR PLACES'!"

****

Mark my words, when a society has to resort to the lavoratory for its humor, the writing is on the wall. *(Alan Bennett)*

Pete Smith had been going to the doctor for several weeks and still he had the worrisome cough. Nothing seemed to work to get rid of it. Finally, he went back to his doctor for the bi-weekly examination. The doctor listened to his cough, nodded and said, "Mr. Smith, I do believe that your cough sounds much better today than it did at your last visit."

"Well, Doctor, it danged well ought to! I been practicing it night and day!"

****

When you think about it, you must admit that most things we worry about never happen.

****

The physician finished his examination of his 100-year-old patient whom he had grown to like. When the old man was dressed, the doctor playfully asked him, "Sir, what's your judgment of today's women?"

"I can't rightly answer that question, Doc," the old man replied. "Y'see, I ain't thought about women for nearly three years now!"

****

A farmer was hammering away in the back yard, stopping now and then to listen to his wife cough, an affliction that was about to drive her crazy. Just then, the doctor came driving up, leaned out the window and asked, "How's the misses?"

"Poorly."

"Is that her coughin', there?"

"Nope. Oh no! This here is a packin' box."

****

Joe Goniff, up in years, had not been feeling well. He decided to visit a doctor where he received a thorough medical examination, after which the doctor said, "Mr. Goniff, I suggest you take life easier, especially sex. You must reduce your sexual activities."

"OK, Doc. But tell me...which part do I give up -- thinking about it or talking about it?"

****

It has been said, and most wisely, that "contraceptives should be used on all conceivable occasions."

There was a sharp lass with a hernia,
Who yelled at the Doctor, "Goldernia,
You can improve my middle
But don't you dare fiddle,
With organs that do not concernia."

****

A man in the hospital was fed his breakfast coffee rectally. Immediately he began to scream. "Too hot?" the nurse asked as she quickly removed the tube.
"No. No...too much sugar!"

****

The receptionist was completing the standard form on a new patient, a man close to eighty years old. "Sir," the receptionist said, "have you lived in this town all your life?"
"Not yet," the old man replied.

****

Worry can sure keep you active...but it won't get you anywhere.

****

"Mr. Petefish," the physician said, "Yours is the strangest complaint I've ever heard. Most men would be delighted. What's so bad about having your virility so high?"
The patient sighed. "Doctor, it's high, all right, high in my head."

****

The doctor entered the hospital room and proceeded to take the pulse of the patient.
"Doctor, I sure do hope you find me sick!"
"That's a bad attitude, Sir. You shouldn't feel that way. Think positively. Why do you say such a thing?"
"Why? Because I'd hate to feel this bad and then have you tell me I'm not sick!"

****

Fortunate is the man who can laugh at himself because he will always be amused.

Dr. Snow, an obstetrician in Meridian, Mississippi, had helped in the birth of three generations from this one family. He happened to meet the grandmother while out walking. They stopped to chat. "Dr. Snow, I got to tell ya that my granddaughter, Norma, is going to have her fourth child. She named the fist three Eenie, Meenie, Minee and she's gonna name this 'un Henry."

"But tell me," asked Dr. Snow. "How come she plans to use Henry for the child's name? Why didn't she just continue the sequence to the end and name him Mo, for Moses or some such name? Mo would have been quite appropriate."

"I'll tell ya why she didn't name him Mo," the grandmother replied spiritedly. "It's because she didn't want no mo', that's why."

****

"Whoever said that women can't take a joke didn't know what the hell they were talking about," said old Doctor Jeffrey Baumgart. "You want proof? Just take a look at their husbands."

****

Some Americans are absolute fatalists. It must have been one of them who penned these revealing lines:

> You have two chances --
> One of getting the germ
> And one of not.
> And if you get the germ
> You have two chances --
> One of getting the disease
> And one of not.
> And if you get the disease
> You have two chances --
> One of dying
> And one of not.
> And if you die --
> Well, you still have two chances.

****

In the psychiatric ward, there were two patients with illusions of grandeur. One of them thought he was Alexander the Great. An attendant asked him, "And just what makes you think you're Alexander the Great?"

"God told me so," replied the patient.

From an adjoining bed came the angry voice of a patient: "I did not!"

Into the Federal Internal Revenue Department in Springfield, Illinois, came a man who had had an automobile accident. His nose was plastered with bandages. He had come to pay his taxes and pulled out a check, prepared to write.

"Had an accident to your nose?" the collector asked, trying to be friendly.

"No," said the taxpayer. "I've been paying through it so long that it's given way under the strain."

****

Music has been called medicine for what ails you. And it is true that some of it is hard to take.

****

Mrs. Edwards, and old friend of Mrs. Peters, met the latter on the street. But Mrs. Edwards was dressed entirely in black. "Did someone in your family pass away?" asked Mrs. Edwards.

"My husband Edgar. He fell out of his boat and drowned. Poor thing. My only consolation is that he left me one hundred thousand dollars."

"One hundred thousand dollars! My oh my. That seems remarkable for a man to accumulate that much money when he could neither read nor write."

"Nor swim," added Mrs. Peters.

****

Patient: "Doc, I had another one of those dreams last night."
Doctor: "Please tell me about it."
Patient: "Well, I dreamed I was all alone in a huge bedroom with 50 beautiful blondes, ten redheads and six brunettes. God, it was horrible."
Doctor: "And just what was so horrible about such an enchanting evening as that?"
Patient: "In the dream, I was a girl."

****

In World War II, a draftee claimed exemption because of poor vision. And the guy brought his wife along as evidence.

****

Here's a neat description of pregnancy: "A woman so swelled up over her mate's work that she puts up a big front."

A woman walked stark naked, totally in the buff, into the psychiatrist's office. When the doctor asked her what her trouble was all about, she replied, "I don't know what to say, exactly, Doctor, but it seems like whenever I walk down the street, I imagine that everybody is looking at me."

****

BEFORE I PROCEED YOU BETTER BRIEF ME
ON YOUR OTHER TICKLISH SPOTS!"

****

In the hill country of Kentucky, they say when a man yells with pain that: "He's squawkin' like a hen layin' a square egg!"

****

One of the best "put-down" stories to come down the pike involves a conceited mayor who kept receiving fan mail from this one man, stuff like: "I think you're the best mayor, the handsomest man, the best citizen in town." Similar letter after letter came to the mayor. Finally this one, from the same person arrived. "Pardon all those letters, and this one, written in crayon, but they won't let me use anything sharp in here."

221

Here's a story that appears in all of our wars. One suspects it started in the Civil War...maybe before that!

One of the most unusual cases of draft-evasion tactics took place during the Korean War. Willie and Jupiter, deciding to outsmart the draft physical, had all their teeth removed the day before the examination was to take place. Reporting to the induction center they took their place in line. Somehow in the confusion a burly garbage collector got in between the two.

As the line of naked men proceeded down the examining room, the physician in charge asked Willie if he wanted to claim exemption from service on the basis of any physical malady.

"Absolutely, doc," said Willie. I haven't got a tooth in my mouth.

The medical man promptly stuck his finger in Willie's mouth and felt all around his gums. "You're right. There isn't a tooth in there. Rejected!"

The garbage man was next in line.

"What about you?" asked the doctor.

"Doc," he said. "You can't draft me. I've gone one of the worst cases of piles you ever saw."

"We'll see about that." Then he made the usual examination with his finger.

"There's no doubt about it," agreed the doctor as the inductee roared with pain. "This is a bad case, alright. Rejected!"

It was Jupiter's turn next.

"I suppose," said the doctor sarcastically, "that you also have a claim for rejection?"

"Hell, no!" cried Jupiter staring at the examining finger. "Just gimme a gun--I'm a fighting fool!"

****

You ask how I'm feelin'? Well, I'll tell ya. I'm fit as a fiddle plumb out of tune.

****

"Did you hear about Jimmy? He had an operation."
"No. How does he feel?"
"Not so derned good. Seems that the doctors removed all of his money."

****

Emetic. A noun the verb of which is much nicer and refined, e.g., "You make me sick and I think I'll emet (vomit)."

222

A disordered patient came running into the psychiatrist's office. He just stood there snapping his fingers and growling in fierce tones. "Calm down, Sir. Take it easy," the physician ordered, "and tell me...why are you doing all that?"

"It keeps away all them elephants."

"But there aren't any elephants around this place, Sir."

"Ah ha! Y'see...it works!"

****

Evers, a beginning life insurance salesman, was delighted. He'd just sold his first policy, a big one for one hundred thousand dollars. He stood before the boss's desk and waited to be congratulated. "You did fine, Evers, but just one thing. You forgot to get a urine sample for our doctor to approve. That's part of the sale. Remember that."

A few days later, Evers struggled into the boss's office and he was staggering under the weight of two huge pails of yellowish liquid.

"What the devil are you hauling in here, Evers?" the boss yelled.

Evers grinned. "I just sold a big group policy," he said.

****

The young man had learned his lesson about AIDS and other venereal diseases. So he went into the drugstore and asked for a dozen condoms. "I can give you a good deal on a gross of them," the druggist said. "They're a lot cheaper that way."

The young man took all 144 condoms and left. But on Monday morning, he stormed into the drugstore shouting, "Mister, there were only 135 condoms in that set and I paid for 144 - a gross."

The druggist apologized. "I beg your pardon, Sir. And I do hope I haven't ruined your weekend."

****

It is no secret that some patients have few friends but plenty of enemas.

****

Did you hear about the two American ladies who had visited France? They were telling of their experiences to a friend. "And do you know," said one lady, "that I spent two weeks in France and didn't once see Cannes."

After which, the third lady replied, "Oh, it was probably due to the change in food and water."

223

Words can cause lots of trouble, or confusion as in the last story. Here's another:

It seems that an old lady was invited to a banquet. In spite of the start of a cold, she went, taking along two Kleenexes that she tucked in the bosom of her low-cut formal gown. Early she used one and later, at the table, she needed another hankie so she reached for it but couldn't find it. She probed deeper and deeper, frantically searching. Everybody was looking at her, wondering what was wrong. Finally, she said, reaching way down in the bodice of her gown, "I know I had two when I left home."

****

"I thought you were Doctor Pierson's patient?"
"I was. But he scared me so much during my last visit that I thought I'd change doctors."
"How did he scare you?
"He told me I was sound as a dollar and, man, that really put me in a panic.""

****

A patient sent her doctor an invitation to her dinner party. In reply, she got a note from him that she could not read. "Gosh. Did he accept or not?" she wondered.
So she took the note to her pharmacist, who was quite used to reading the doctor's writing. He took the note, left to go to the back room and returned with a small box and said: "That'll be thirty dollars, please."

****

The wife of a hospital intern knew a few medical terms. In fact, she considered herself a pretty good diagnostician. One day, she called the family physician about her aged father. "I need the name of a good urinologist," she said, "a gentile-urinary doctor. I figure my Pa will have to be castorized on account of last year they told him he had an enlarged prostitute."

****

"You don't beat around the bush, do you, Doc?" the patient said as the doctor laid down required changes to his lifestyle in no uncertain terms. "You're about as subtle as a rhinoceros in heat."

224

·ᗩLEITCH·

"YOUR CONDITION? WELL, LET ME PUT IT THIS
WAY ... THANKS TO YOU I MAY BE ABLE
TO AFFORD LIABILITY INSURANCE AFTER
ALL".

****

Painfully thin was Lena;
When she bought her new vacuum cleaner.
    She got in the way
    Of the suction one day,
And Lena since then ain't been seena.

****

A high school girl experienced some female distress and her
mother brought her to the town physician. He examined the young
lady then asked the girl's mother: "Has your daughter ever gone
to a gynecologist?"
"Nope. Don't think so. She only went far as high school."

****

Then there was the lovely lady who had just had quadruplets.
Her friend came to visit her. "Wasn't it hard to pick four names for
those lovely kids you just had?" the friend asked.
"Not at all. It was easy," said the new mother. "I named two of
them just as I planned to do. Then I added two more names. Now
it's Adolph, Rudolph, Getoff and Stayoff!"

225

Back in Danny Kaye's heyday, the THETA KAPPA PSI fraternity newsletter offered this masterpiece of illiteration with the suggestion that Danny Kaye exercise his vocal chords sing-song-singing it.

Medical Whimsey

Pellagra is the predestined penalty plying people who perversely persist in partaking of pale, preserved, potted, purified, polished, pickled, pared, pauperized, pathetic, pallid, puerile, paltry, parboiled, puny, pusillanimous, pediculous, piddling, prostrated, proprietary, and patent pap, pathetically passing as provender among penurious or parsimonious paupers and a perverted populace, due probably to paucity of pence or perspicacity, or possibly to a pernicious predilection for palatable provisions. Pellagrous patients provide a pitiful pathologic picture of palsy and paralysis, and are perculiarly prone to pruritus, porphyrinuria, parethesia, paralogia, and paranoia. Not to protract this platitudinous peroration, please preach and propagate the policy to our procrastinating and perishing population, that they prevent pellagra by the pleasant prophylaxis of polishing off plenty of peas, potatoes, pot-likker, parsnips, parsley, paprika, pancakes, porridge, pears, pie, pineapple, peppers, papayas, pawpaws, and proteins as pork, pigeons, pheasant, pancreas, and pemmican.

****

An elderly gentleman now ninety years old, said, "If I'd known that I would live this long I'd have taken a lot better care of myself."

****

Did you hear about Sally, the health nut? Well, she insisted upon eating all her vegetables raw...until the cafe owner insisted that she put her clothes on.

****

Girls have got to be careful when they accept invitations to attend college football games. Consider the case of the young lady who attended an Illinois/Iowa football game and came away from it with a very bad case of *"athlete's foetus."*

****

One time a fellow walked into the psychiatrist's office and announced, "Doctor Jones, I promise that if you can cure me of my delusions, I'll grant you eternal life."

The psychiatrist was endeavoring to find out how the farm wife spent her days. Patiently, the country lady detailed her activities from early morning until bedtime. There was cooking, baby-tending, cleaning, washing, ironing, mending, chicken-feeding, canning, gardening, dusting, dishwashing and so on.

"Yes, yes," the psychiatrist interrupted impatiently, "but your free time. Please tell me what you do with your free time!"

The lady hesitated, thinking, then nodded and said, "I go to the toilet!"

****

In coronary specialty circles, they say that the very first heart transplant survivor was...Richard the Lion-Hearted.

****

On a spring day in the play area of the mental institution, three sufferers were amusing themselves. One kept pawing the air furiously while the second fellow dipped his hands as though he were scooping water. The third guy was busy waving his arms wildly in circles.

An attendant came by and asked the first man, "Hey, Bub, what are you doing"

"Picking stars."

"And you?" he asked the second man.

"I'm pickin' up the stars that that jerk drops."

"And how about you, Mister Scooper. What the hell you doin'?"

The third inmate giggled. "Hell, Man, a guy has got to do something around here to keep from going nuts."

****

A new kid in the house is always a great source of excitement for the family, especially the other children. After the new baby arrived home, the little girl ran to tell her friend of the new arrival. "Is the kid going to stay?" asked her friend.

"I guess so, he's got all his clothes off."

"How'd you know it's a he?"

"Well, I heard the folks talkin' and Ma said he had her features and Papa's fixtures."

"Who was it brought the baby?"

"Dr. Lloyd."

"Oh yeah. We take from him, too."

There is a story going the rounds in medical circles about a man who complained of constant fatigue and depression. The doctor told him there was nothing wrong that a stimulant, in moderation, would not aid. "A bit of whiskey, now and then, and you'll feel like a new man," the doctor told him.

"But, Doctor. In my church we forbid alcohol. We are all Prohibitionists."

"I'll fix it so the family will never know. I'll send you a jug of the right stuff and you take it in hot water four or five times a day."

"But, Doctor, if I send for hot water, they'll know something is wrong."

"Don't worry. Just keep a tea kettle in your room and when you want hot water, send the kettle down and let them fill it for your 'tea'."

A week later the doctor called the man's home to see how things were going. Everybody was excited. "Oh, Doctor," the patient's daughter exclaimed. "He seems okay physically, but he's gone plumb nuts. He's been sending for hot water for his teas, six and seven times a day."

****

Puberty. In the male, a voice-lowering and a penis-raising time. In the female it is a time of chest-raising and flibberttygibbetting!

****

Is it possible that doctors sometimes overdo this exercise-after-operations regime? This patient thought so:

The surgeon told the fellow: "We insist on the patient getting on his feet as soon as possible after the operation. Now, on the first day, I want you out of bed and walking around the room for five minutes. OK? On the second day, you get up and walk around ten minutes. OK? On the third day, you will walk around one hour. Got that? Any questions?"

"Just one, Doc," said the patient. "For the operation itself...is it okay if I lie down?"

****

Never describe a woman as "fat"...say she's short for her weight.

****

Gestation: A developing pregnancy caused by a semi-religious condition...a holey condom.

The doctor had just delivered the twelfth child to Mrs. Truit. He called her husband outside the delivery room and said, "Now the next time you feel like having sex with your wife, I want you to ask yourself, 'Can I support yet another child?'"

"Doctor," said the new father, "when I feel like propagatin' I feel fer damn sure like I could support the whole damn state of Missouri."

****

It's very important that you keep busy, Mrs. Endicott, the doctor told her. "You're physical condition seems good for a woman eighty-five years of age. But I do think you should show more interest in the world around you."

"Oh, but I do, Doctor! I have lots of fun with my five boyfriends."

"Boyfriends, Mrs. Endicott?"

"Yep! My friend Will Power eases me out of bed every morning. Then I sit down to breakfast with that nice gentleman, Charlie Horse. After breakfast and along toward noon, Arthur Itis comes along and I go to lunch with him. We do the town hitting joint after joint and by that time I'm so derned tired that I got to bed. Yep! I'm real glad to bundle up with Ben Gay. There's a fifth gent who seems real interested in me but I don't much care for him."

"What is his name?" the doctor asked.

"Al Sheimer! Nasty guy!"

****

And then there was the fellow who greeted his friend with this: "Man oh man, I sure hope I'm sick."

"Hope you're sick!" exclaimed his friend. "That's a terrible thing to say."

"Well, I mean that I'd sure as hell hate to feel this bad and then find out that there's nothing wrong with me."

****

Sex. The silly, ludicrous and often hilarious way that humans (and others) propagate their kind.

****

The story is circulating around Presbyterian Hospital in Chicago that there is now a statistic that says one out of four people in the Untied States is unbalanced. Now that is no cause for concern...no cause at all...unless you have three friends you think are perfectly normal.

They tell a real cute story down in Kentucky about a girl, the birth of whose child was imminent, so near that, rushed to the hospital she never quite made it. She delivered on the hospital lawn. But the family got a bill for $1,000!

The husband wrote the hospital and said how unfair it was to charge the regular fee when the delivery room was the front lawn. Pretty soon a new bill arrived that stated: "GREENS FEE: $400."

****

Perhaps the most popular and oft-given remedy for the common cold is...advice!

****

There was a young fellow named Weir,
Who hadn't an atom of fear.
    He indulged a desire
    To touch a live wire.
(Most any last line will do here).

****

"SINCE YOU'VE PASSED A CARDIOVASCULAR FITNESS TEST, DO YOU SUPPOSE YOU MIGHT AT LEAST TAKE OUT THE GARBAGE?"

6

EARLY AMERICAN MEDICAL HUMOR

Patent medicines were numerous and a popular cure in the nineteenth century. Here's a satire on them as revealed in *Doesticks, What He Says*, by Mortimer Thompson (1831-1875).

A new Patent Medicine Operation.

Congratulate me -- I am immortalized, and I've done it myself. My name will be handed down to posterity as that of a universal benefactor. The hand which hereafter writes upon the record of Fame, the names of Ayer, Sands, Townsend, Moffat, Morrison, and Brandreth, must also inscribe, side by side with these distinguished appellations, the no less brilliant cognomen of the undying Doesticks.

Emulous of the deathly notoriety which has been acquired by the medicinal worthies just mentioned, *I* also resolved to achieve a name and a fortune in the same reputable and honest manner.

Bought a gallon of tar, a cake of beeswax, and a firkin of lard, and in twenty-one hours I presented to the world the first batch of *"Doesticks' Patent, Self-Acting, Four-Horse Power Balsam,"* designed to cure all diseases of mind, body, or estate, to give strength to the weak, money to the poor, bread and butter to the hungry, boots to the barefoot, decency to blackguards, and common sense to the Know-Nothings. It acts physically, morally, mentally, psychologically, physiologically, and geologically, and it is intended to make our sublunary sphere a blissful paradise, to which Heaven itself shall be but a side-show.

I have not yet brought it to absolute perfection, but even now it acts with immense force, as you will perceive by the accompanying testimonials and records of my own individual experience. You will observe that I have not resorted to the ususal manner of preparing certificates: which is, to be certain that all those intended for Eastern circulation shall seem to come from some formerly unheard-of place in the West, while those sent to the West shall be dated at some place forty miles east of sun-rise. But I send to *you*, as representing the western country, a certificate from an Oregon farmer.

"Dear Sir: The land composing my farm has hitherto been so poor that a Scotchman couldn't get his living off it; and so stony that we had to slice our potatoes and plant them edgeways; but, hearing of your balsam, I put some on the corner of a ten-acre lot, surrounded by a rail-fence, and in the morning I found the rocks had entirely disappeared -- a neat stone wall encircled the field, and the rails were split into even wood and piled up symmetrically in my back yard.

Put half an ounce into the middle of a huckleberry swamp -- in two days it was cleared off, planted with corn and pumpkins, and had a row of peach trees in full bloom through the middle.

As an evidence of its tremendous strength, I would state that it drew a striking likeness of my eldest daughter -- drew my youngest boy out of the mill-pond -- drew a blister all over his stomach -- drew a load of potatoes four miles to market, and eventually drew a prize of ninety-seven dollars in the State Lottery.

And the effect upon the inhabitants hereabout has been so wonderful, that they have opened their eyes to the good of the country, and are determined to vote for a Governor who is opposed to frosts in the middle of June, and who will make a positive law against freshets, hail-storms, and the seventeen-year locusts."

There, isn't that *some?*

****

Opie Read (1852-1939) was one of the frontier-humorist breed whose *Arkansas Traveler* (from which the following article is taken) reveals a good indirect view of what life was like on the American frontier.

Pleased with the Chills

Down in certain sections of the Mississippi River bottoms there is such an air of unconcern that the first thought of a traveler is: "These people are too lazy to entertain a hope." It is, however, not wholly a condition of laziness that produces such an appearance of indolence. Laziness may play its part, and, moreover, may play it well, but it cannot hope to assume the leading role. What, then, is the principal actor? Chills. There are men in those bottoms who were born with a chill and who have never shaken it off.

Some time ago while riding through the Muscadine neighborhood, I came upon a man sitting on a log near the roadside. He was sallow and lean, with sharp knob check bones and with hair that looked like soiled cotton. The day was intensely hot, but he was sitting in the sun, although near him a tangled grapevine cast a most inviting shade.

"Good-morning," said I, reigning up my horse.

"Hi."

"You live here, I suppose."

"Jest about."

"Why don't you sit over there in the shade?"

"Will when the time comes."

"What do you mean by when the time comes?"

"When the fever comes on."

"Having chills, are you?"

"Sorter."

"How long have you had them?"

"Forty-odd year."

"How old are you?"

"Forty odd year."

"Been shaking all your life, eh?"

"Only half my life; fever was on the other half."

"Why don't you move away from here?"

"Becaze I've lived here so long that I'm afeerd that I might not have good health nowhar else."

"Gracious alive, do you mean to say that having chills all the time is good health?"

"Wall, health mout be wuss. Old Nat Sarver moved up in the hills some time ago, was tuck down putty soon with some new sort of disease and didn't live more'n a week. Don't b'lieve in swappin' off suthin' that I'm used to fur suthin' I don't know nothin' about. Old-fashioned, every-day chills air good enough for me. Some folks, when they git a little up in the world, mout want to put on airs with dyspepsia and bronkichus, and glanders and catarrh, but, as I 'lowed to my wife the other night, old chills and fever war high enough fur us yit awhile. A chill may have its drawbacks, but it has its enjoyments too."

"I don't see how anything about a chill can be enjoyable."

'Jest owin' to how you air raised, as the feller says. When I have a chill it does me a power of good to stretch, and I tell you that a fust-rate stretch when a feller is in the humor ain't to be sneezed at. I'd leave watermilon most any time to have a good stretch. High-o-hoo!" He gasped, threw out his legs, threw back his arms and stretched himself across the log. "It's sorter like the itch," he went on. "The itch has its drawbacks, but what a power of good it does a man to scratch! Had a uncle who cotch the itch in the army and he lay thar and scratched and smiled and scratched agin. In order to keep up with the demand of the occasion he sprinkled a lot of sand in his bed and tuck off all his clothes, so that every time he turned he'd be scratched all over. He kep' this up till the itch killed him, but he died a-scratchin' and a-smilin' and I reckon he was about as happy a dead man as every lived. Wall, my fever is comin' on now and I reckon I'll git up thar under the shade."

He moved into the shade and stretched himself again.

"How long will your fever last?" I asked.

"Wall, I don't know exackly; three hours, mebby."

"Then what?"

"Wall, I'll funter around awhile, chop up a little wood to git a bite to eat with, swap a hoss with some feller, mebby, and then fix myself for another chill."

"Have you much of a family?"

"Wife and grown son. He's about the ablest chiller in the country; w'y, when he got a rale good chill on he can take hold of a tree and shake off green persimmons. W'y he wins all the money the folks have got, shakin' dice. Wall, have you got to go?"

"Yes."

"Wait till my fever cools down a little, and I'll beat you outen that nag you're ridin'."

"No, I don't care to walk."

"Good-bye, then. When you git tired livin' up thar among them new-fangled diseases, come down here whar everthing is old-fashioned and honest."

****

Finley Peter Dunne, the creator of Martin Dooley, was born in Chicago on July 10, 1867, of Irish immigrant parents. Not much of a student (he finished last in his high school class). He went to work for a Chicago newspaper and published his first column in 1892. A year later, his internationally famous Irish-American character, Martin Dooley, appeared in a column. From then on, with increasing popularity here and in England, "Mr. Dooley" stole his way into American hearts and, especially, the American funny bone.

Mr. Dooley on the Grip

Mr. Dooley was discovered making a seasonable beverage, consisting of one part syrup, two parts quinine, and fifteen parts strong water.

"What's the matter?" asked Mr. McKenna.

"I have th' lah gr-rip," said Mr. Dooley, blowing his nose and wiping his eyes. "Bad cess to it! Oh, me poor back! I feels as if a dhray had run over it. Did ye iver have it? Ye did not? Well, ye're lucky. Ye're a lucky man.

"I wint to McGuire's wake las' week. They gave him a dacint sind-off. No porther. An' himself looked natural, as fine a corpse as iver Gavin layed out. Gavin tould me so himsilf. He was as proud iv McGuire as if he owned him. Fetched half th' town in to look at him, an' give ivry wan iv thim cards. He near frightened ol' man Dugan into a faint. 'Misther Dugan, how old a-are ye?' 'Sivinity-five, thanks be,' says Dugan. 'Thin,' says Gavin, 'take wan iv me cards,' he says. 'I hope ye'll not forget me,' he says.

"'Twas there I got th' lah grip. Lastewise, it is me own opinion iv it, tho th' doctor said I swalled a bug. It don't seem right, Jawn, f'r th' McGuires is a clane fam'ly; but th' docthor said a bug got into me system. 'What short of bug?' says I. 'A lah grip bug,' he says. 'Ye have Mickrobes in ye're lungs,' says he. 'What's thim?' says I? 'Thim's th' lah grip bugs,' says he.'Ye took wan in, an' warmed it,' he says, 'an' it has growed an' multiplied till ye're system does be full if thim,' he says, 'millions iv thim,' he says, 'marchin' an' counter-marchin' through ye.' 'Glory be to the saints!' says I. 'Had I better swallow some insect powdher?' I says. 'Some iv thim in me head has a fallin' out, an' is throwin' bricks.' 'Foolish man,' says he. 'Go to bed,' he says, 'an' lave thim alone,' he says; 'whin they find who they're in,' he says, 'they'll quit ye.'

"So I wint to bed, an' waited while th' Mickrobes had fun with me. Mondah all iv them was quiet but thim in me stummick. They stayed up late dhrinkin' an' carousin' an' dancin' jigs till wurruds come up between th' Kerry Mickrobes an' thim fr'm Wexford; an' th' whole party wint over to me left lung, where they cud get th' air, an' had it out. Th' nex' day th' little Mickrobes made a tobaggan slide iv me spine; an' manetime some Mickrobes that was wurkin' f' th' tilliphone comp'ny got it in their heads that me legs was poles, an' put their spikes an' climbed all night long.

"They was tired out th' next' day till about five o'clock, whin thim that was in me head began flushin' out th' rooms; an' I knew theer was goin' to be doin's in th' top flat. What did them Mickrobes do but invite all th' other Mickrobes in f'r th' ev'nin. They all come. Oh, by gar, they was not wan iv thim stayed away. At six o'clock they begin to move fr'm me shins to me throat. They come in platoons an' squads an' dhroves. Some iv thim brought along brass bands, an' more thin wan hundred thousand iv thim dhruv through me pipes on dhrays. A trolley line was started up me back, and iv'ry car run into a wagon-load if scrapiron at th' base if me skull.

"Th' Mickrobes in me head must've done thimselves proud. They tipped over th' chairs an' tables; an' in less time thin it takes to tell, th' whole party was at it. They'd been a hurlin' game in th' back iv me skull, an' th' young folks was dancin' breakdowns an' havin' leppin matches in me forehead; but they all stopt, to mix in. Oh, 'twas a grand shindig--tin millions iv men, women, an childher rowlin' on th' flure, hands an' feet goin', ice-picks an' hurlin' sticks, clubs, brick-bats, flyin' in th' air! How many iv thim was kilt I niver knew; f'r I wint as daft as a hen, an' dhreamt iv organizin' a Mickrobe Campaign Club that'd sweep th' prim'ries, an' maybe go acrost an' free Ireland. Whin I woke up, me legs was as weak as a day-old baby's, an' me poor head impty as a cobbler's purse. I want no more iv thim. Give me anny bug fr'm a cockroach to an aygle, save an' excipt thim West if Ireland Fenians, th' Mickrobes."

Even today, physicians are called to treat fleas on their patients; and occasionally, bedbugs. Hence, it is enlightening to review some early treatments used to evacuate these pests. Here are two treatments described by John Phoenix (George H. Derby) back in 1856. As he would say, those treatments for fleas and bedbugs were *some*!

A Sure Cure for Fleas

The following recipe from the writings of Miss Hannah More, may be found useful to your readers:

In a climate where the attacks of fleas are a constant source of annoyance, any method which will alleviate them becomes a *desideratum.* It is, therefore, with pleasure I make known the following recipe, which I am assured has been tried with efficacy.

Boil a quart of tar until it becomes quite thin. Remove the clothing, and before the tar becomes perfectly cool, with a broad flat brush, apply a thin, smooth coating to the entire surface of the body and limbs. While the tar remains soft, the flea becomes entangled in its tenacious folds, and is rendered perfectly harmless; but it will soon form a hard, smooth coating, entirely impervious to his bite. Should the coating crack at the knee or elbow joints, it is merely necessary to retouch it slightly at those places. The whole coat should be renewed every three or four weeks. This remedy is sure, and having the advantage of simplicity and economy, should be generally known.

So much for Miss More. A still simpler method of preventing the attacks of these little pests, is one which I have lately discovered myself;--in theory only--I have not yet put it into practice. On feeling the bite of a flea, thrust the part bitten immediately into boiling water. The heat of the water destroys the insect and instantly removes the pain of the bite....

The Rip Van Winkle Bug

A few evenings since, in the "private crib" of one of our exchanges, there was a learned dissertation, subject, "Bed-bugs, and their Remarkable Tenacity of Life." One asserted of his own knowledge that they could be boiled, and then come to life. Some had soaked them for hours in turpentine without any fatal consequences. Old Hanks, who had been listening as an outsider, here gave in his experience in corroboration of the facts. Says he, "Some years ago I took a bed-bug to an iron-foundry, and dropping it into a ladle where the melted iron was, had it run into a skillet. Well, my old woman used that skillet pretty constant for the last six years, and here the other day it broke all to smash; and what do you think, gentlemen, that 'ere insect just walked out of his hole, where he'd been layin' like a frog in a rock, and made tracks for his old roost upstairs! But," added he, by way of parenthesis, "he looked mighty pale."

****

Back in 1877, twelve years after our Civil War, J.M. Bailey, known as the Danbury-News Man, published a collection of his newspaper articles under the title: *They All Do It: or, Mr. Miggs of Danbury and His Neighbors.* He relates the case of a man accidentally scalped and how the medical experts of that day replaced (somewhat!) the lost tresses.

An Astonishing Cure.

Here is something remarkable. A woman in New-Haven was recently bereft of her scalp by the idiosyncrasies of a shaft and belt. The doctors saw, that, to remedy the evil, they would have to recourse to transplanting; and so they actually succeeded in getting a sufficient number of pieces from other peoples' heads to give this unfortunate woman a new scalp. We hope those New-Haven doctors used more discretion than did he who attended a man named Finlay, who met with a similar accident in Oriskany, N.Y., some thirteen years ago. Bits of scalp from seventeen different persons were secured by this doctor, and adroitly stitched to the head of Mr. Finlay. When it was done, people came miles to see Finlay's head; and Finlay himself, with his checker-board cranium, was the happiest man in Oriskany. But, when the capillary glands got in working-order, and the hair commenced to grow, the top of that man's head presented the most extraordinary spectacle on record. The doctor, who was half the time in liquor, had consulted expediency rather than judgment, and secured that new scalp without any reference to future developments. We never saw anything like it. Here was a tuft of yellow hair, and next to it a bit of black, and then a flame of red, and a little like silk, and more like tow, with brown hair, and gray hair, and sandy hair, and cream-colored hair, scattered over his entire skull. And what a mad man that Finlay was and nobody could blame him. He would stand up against the barn for an hour at a time, and sob and swear. It was very fortunate that the doctor was dead. He went off two weeks before the blue ague, which is a mild sort of disease. Finlay kept his hair cut short; but that didn't make any difference. Then he tried dyes; but they only made matters worse. Then he got a wig, and this covered up the deformity; but sometimes at church he would get asleep, and the wig would fall off, and make the children cry. Once, at the county fair, he fell asleep, and the wig dropped off; and the committee on domestic goods, when they came around, stood in front of Finlay's head for some five

237

minutes rapt in delight. They then immediately decided that it was the most ingenious piece of patchwork in the list, and never discovered the mistake until they attempted to pin the premium card to it. At that Finlay awoke, and knocked down the chairman of the committee, and chased the others out of the building. We hope those New-Haven doctors have been more particular, as it is not a subject to trifle with.

****

David Ross Locke (1833-1888) was a favorite humorist of the American people and, especially, of Abraham Lincoln who kept a copy of *The Nasby Papers* on his desk. Locke used phonetic spelling -- very popular back then -- and played the part of a Southern sympathizer living in the North...they were called Copperhead Democrats. His character, Petroleum V. Nasby, is one of the most unredeemed scoundrels in American Literature.

Shows Why He Should Not Be Drafted
August 6, 1862

I see in the papers last nite, that the Government hez institooted a draft, and that in a few weeks, sum hunderds uv thousands uv peesable citizens will be dragged to the tented feeld. I know not wat uthers may do, but ez fer me, I can't go. Upon a rigid eggsaminashen uv my fizzlekle man, I find it wood be wus ner madnis fer me 2 undertake a campane, to-wit:

1. I'm bald-headid, and hev bin obliged to ware a wig these 22 yeres.

2. I hev dandruff in wat scanty hair still hangs around my venerable temples.

3. I hev a chronic katarr.

4. I hev lost, sence Stanton's order to draft, the use uv wun eye entirely, and hev cronic inflammashen in the other.

5. My teeth is all unsound, my palit aint eggsactly rite, and I hev hed bronkeetis 31 yeres last Joon. At present I hev a koff, the paroxisms uv wich is friteful 2 behold.

6. I'm holler-chestid, am short-winded, and hev alluz hed panes in my back and side.

7. I am afflictid with kronic diarrear and kostivniss. The money I hev paid er Jayneses karminnytiv balsam and pills wood astonish almost ennybody.

8. I am rupcherd in 9 places, and am entirely enveloped with trusses.

9. I hev verrykose vanes, hev a white swellin on wun leg and a fever sore on the uther--also wun leg is shorter than tother, though I handle it so expert that noboddy never noticed it.

10. I hev korns and bunyons on both feet, wich wood prevent me from marchin.

I don't suppose that my political opinions, wich are ferninst the prossekooshn uv this unconstooshnel war, wood hev any wate with a draftin orfiser, but the above reesons why I cant go, will, I maik no doubt, be suffishent.

Petroleum V. Nasby

****

Hospitals for Liars
Anonymous
(About 1870)

A few days ago I visited the fairly recently established infirmary for liars in a quiet location in upstate New York. Since it was known that a representative of the TIMES was due, I was met at the door by a pleasant-faced gentleman, who spoke with a slight German accent and introduced himself as the Assistant Superintendent.

"Will you kindly walk this way?" he said. After I had inscribed my name in the Visitors' Book, he began to explain the system under which the infirmary for the mendacious operates.

"It is very simple," he said. "The theory of the Institution is that the habit of mendacity, which in many cases becomes chronic, is a disease, like habitual inebriety. It can generally be cured. We take the liar who voluntarily submits himself to our treatment, and for six months we encourage him in lying. We surround him with liars, his equals and superiors in skill, and cram him with falsehood until he is saturated.

"By this time, the reaction has set in. The patient is usually starved for the truth. He is prepared to welcome the second course of treatment. For the next half year the opposite course is pursued. The satiated and disgusted liar is surrounded by truthful attendants, and by force of example and moral influence, brought to understand how much more creditable it is to say the thing which *is* than the thing *which is not*. Then we send him back into the world. I will show you how our patients live. We will go first, if you please, through the left wing of the hospital, where the saturating process may be observed."

He led the way across a hall into a large room, comfortably furnished and occupied by two dozen or more gentlemen who sat or stood in groups, engaged in animated talk. Near one group, I overheard parts of the conversation.

"My rod creaked and bent double," a stout red-faced gentleman was saying, "and the birch spun like a teetotum. I tell you, if Pierre

239

Chaveau hadn't had the presence of mind to grip the most convenient part of my trousers with the boat hook, I should have been dragged into the lake in two seconds or less. Well, sir, we fought sixty-nine minutes by actual timetaking, and when I had him in and had got him back to the hotel, he tipped the scale, the speckled beauty did, at thirty-seven pounds and eleven-sixteenths, whether you believe it or not."

"Nonsense," said a quiet little gentleman who sat opposite. "That is impossible."

The first speaker looked flattered at this and flushed with pleasure. "Nevertheless," he retorted, "it's a fact, on my honor as a sportsman. Why do you say it's impossible?"

"Because," said the other, calmly, "it is an ascertained scientific fact, as every true fisherman in this room knows perfectly well, that there are no trout in Lake Mooselemagunticook weighing under half a hundred pounds."

"Certainly not," put in a third speaker. "The bottom of the lake is of a sieve formation. All fish smaller than the fifty-pounders fall through."

"Why doesn't the water drop through, too?" asked the stout patient, in a triumphant tone.

"It used to," replied the quiet gentleman gravely, "until the Maine Legislature passed an act preventing it."

****

Wonderful Hair-Reproducer
(Author Unknown)

Dr. _____, of New York, sent us a cake of his Onguent, with the modest request to "puff it, and send the bill."

Venerable and far-sighted capillary producer! We do, and more too. Your Onguent is a big thing. Although in small cakes, it is nevertheless a colossal item. We tried it. Following the printed directions given, we made a lather and applied the brush. The lather was mixed in a glass dish, and in four minutes a beautiful hair, all shades of color, had started from the dish. We applied some to our face, and it took four swift-working barbers to cut down and mow away as fast as the beard grew. We put a little on the toe of each boot, and in an hour they looked like Zouave mustaches. We put some on a crowbar, and it is covered with long, curly hair like a buffalo, and in the coldest weather it can be used without mittens. A little on the carriage-pole started the hair on it like moss. We dropped some on the stove, and as the fire was kindled the hair started, and the hotter the stove became, the faster grew the hair, till the smell of the burnt hair became so powerful as to drive all from the room. The stove was set in the barn, and it can't be seen now, as the hair is literally stacked upon it. Only one application. A little applied on a wagon-tire has in five days started a vigorous crop, and now the wagon can be driven over a plank-road and not make the least noise, so well are the wheels covered with soft hair. Only one application -- dollar a cake. We skinned a goose, put on some of the Onguent, and in two hours the feather-grower was enveloped in hair like a squirrel, and was seen this morning trying to climb a shagbark hickory in the back-yard. A little applied to the inkstand has given it a coat of bristles, making a splended pen-wiper at little cost. We applied the lather to a tenpenny nail, and the nail is now the handsomest lather-brush you ever saw, with a beautiful growth of soft hair at the end of it, some five or six feet in length. Only a dollar a cake! Applied to door stones, it does away with the use of a mat. Applied to a floor, it will cause to grow therefrom hair sufficient for a Brussels carpet. A little of this Onguent lather was accidentally dropped on the head of our cane, which has been perfectly bald for over ten years, and immediately a thick growth of hair formed, completely covering it, compelling us to shave the head twice a week. Only a dollar a bottle--directions thrown in. A little weak lather sprinkled over a barn makes it impervious to wind, rain, or cold. It is good to put inside of children's cradles--sprinkle on sidewalks, anything, where luxuriant grass is wanted for use or ornament. We put a little on the head of navigation, and a beautiful hair covered it. A little on the mouth of Mississippi river started hair there resembling the finest red-top grass, in which cows, sheep, pigs, hogs, snipes, woodcock, and young ducks graze with keen relish. Only a dollar a cake. Sent by mail to any address. One application will grow a luxuriant mustache for a boy. One dollar a cake. Samson used it.

****

Back in 1895, in California, there was a mythical organization of the medical profession called, *The Antiseptic Club!* Its activities were labeled as *The Transactions of the Antiseptic Club*, and a book was published by that name. The club secretary was Dr. Albert Abrams, M.D. The author, "A member of the San Francisco Medical Profession," kept excellent records of the doings of the "Society." Here is an example of his records of various papers delivered by members of the society.

The next business in order was a paper by Dr. Abductor Pollicis, on "The Climate of California." He humbly apologized to the president and members of the club for reading a paper on this hackneyed subject. He knew that braver men than he had been before annihilated for the same offense, but hoped they would be able to endure a slight infliction of this kind. When he said braver men he referred to those gray-haired veterans who succumbed to

241

the exhilarating effects of our climate and whisky. His first knowledge of the glorious climate of California dated back to the time when he was born, and it was then, for the first time in his life, that he appreciated it. As a child, owing to his ignorance in the methods of breathing--for he did not breathe as intelligently as other children--he contracted the colic by accidentally swallowing a piece of "Cliff-House fog." The doctor who was called to attend him was represented to have been a remarkably clever man, inasmuch as he had won several big prizes in the Louisiana Lottery. He was a great favorite among the ladies on account of his winning ways; but the speaker did not especially admire his treatment. It consisted in the main of swallowing a lot of blotting-paper on the principle that the latter would absorb the moisture of which fog was largely composed. He remembered, although the details were blotted from his memory, that the physician gave his mother a fog-horn to blow, and on his mother's inquiring the reason for this singular procedure, replied that as long as the fog was thick there was danger. He recalled blowing the horn at certain times to relieve his poor mother, and they only ceased blowing it when they concluded, by the absence of pains, that the fog had become dissipated. The doctor who had insisted upon his swallowing blotting-paper was theoretically correct when he argued that blotting-paper facilitated absorption in the intestines, but it was a method of treatment that was quite heroic.

Since the event just narrated, Dr. Pollicis had developed epilepsy, in consequence of ingesting San Francisco fog by accident; but he cured himself completely by buying his clothes ready-made, since which time he has never had a fit.

****

Misleading and false testimonials must have been a problem back in San Francisco at the turn of the century. Here is a satire of those hokey testimonials -- delivered in 1895 by the Antiseptic Club's members.

Testimonial No. 1

"Your purgine is a dandy. One of my patients was so constipated that he had to swallow keys to open his bowels. I take your purgine twice daily. I am a surgeon in active practice, and have two successful operations a day."

Testimonial No. 2

"I am twenty-six years of age and wear whiskers. For over two years I have been troubled with eczema of the beard, which I attributed to the irritating action of the wind. After using your wonderful lubricator for the whiskers, the passage of the wind is so much facilitated that I no longer suffer from eczema."

Testimonial No. 3

"One of my patients, the human ostrich in a circus, who digests stones, nails, glass, and other nouns, has been a sufferer from indigestion for many months. By means of your 'Diejustyet' he is able to assimilate milk and to continue in his occupation of digesting stones, nails, glass, and other nouns."

Testimonial No. 4

"Your diarrhea medicine is a lulu. To show you how it acts: I happened to get a drop of it in my watch and it stopped it at once. While walking down the street yesterday I saw a run-away horse. With rare presence of mind I bethought myself of your medicine, a bottle of which I had in my pocket. After throwing it at the animal I stopped it immediately."

Testimonial No. 5

"I have used your antifat remedy steadily for over thirty years and wouldn't be without it. One of my patients profited by your remedy. While in jail he was given a bottle of your medicine by a friend, and three days later he effected his escape through the waste-pipe."

Testimonial No. 6

"Your hair-restorer is fine. Since using three bottles my hair has all come out. One bottle will restore old hair mattresses. It will also restore the hair in old tooth and hair brushes if properly used."

Testimonial No. 7

"I have been cured by the Keeley cure for alcoholism three times, but nevertheless continued to use whisky. Thanks to your 'Anti-Whiskine,' I have lost my appetite for whisky entirely, and now drink nothing stronger than gin."

Testimonial No. 8

"I have used your fat-reducer until now I am almost a skeleton. The students find me very interesting for demonstration purposes in my lectures on osteology."

"As you know, the Tower of Pisa is bent with age. I happened to ascend the tower not long ago, and what was my surprise to discover that the tower had suddenly become straight! In seeking an explanation for this phenomenon I found that a bottle of your 'Rejuvenator' had fallen from my pocket and its contents were promiscuously distributed. It was only after the medicine had evaporated that the tower leaned as before."

Testimonial No. 10

"Before practicing medicine I was a teacher of penmanship. My success in practice being hampered by the legibility of my prescriptions, I willingly applied myself to a study of your code of hieroglyphics. What was the result? To-day I am a man of affluence, enveloped in all the mysticism which a credulous public respects and pays for."

****

In 1896, Clifton Johnson published a fascinating book of New England folk customs and sayings with the title, *"What They Say in New England: A Book of Signs, Sayings, and Superstition."* There was a chapter of medical cures, folk remedies of that time, some of which persist until today. A selection from the chapter, *"Medicinal,"* appears below.

MEDICINAL

When you have rheumatism, carry a potato in your pocket. The potato will become hard after a time, and believers in its virtues affirm that this is because of the rheumatism it has absorbed.

When a child has fits, the parents sometimes get a puppy for the child to play with and sleep with. The belief is that the dog will take the disease, and that as the dog grows worse the child will grow better. When the dog dies, the child will be completely cured.

Carry a horse-chestnut in your pocket and you will not be troubled by rheumatism.

The child that wears a black silk cord around its neck will not have the croup.

Wear an eelskin around your waist to keep off rheumatism. Some say they had rather have the rheumatism.

Carry an onion in your pocket, and you will not have fits.

Carry camphor-gum, and you will not catch small-pox or contagious diseases.

"I had a great-aunt that used to have the cramp terrible till some

244

one told her to tie a cotton string around her ankle. After that she never had a cramp to the end of her days."

If a bald-headed man washes his head with sage tea, it will make a new growth of hair come out.

The use of tobacco is believed to prevent one's taking diseases.

If a sick person itches, he will get well.

If he is cross, he will get well.

"That isn't always so. There was a man in our town who was very sick, and his wife did something or other he didn't like, and he sat right up in bed and swore at her, and the next instant he fell over dead."

Put the first aching tooth you have pulled in a glass of whiskey. Then drink the whiskey, and you will never have occasion to have another tooth pulled because it aches.

Carry an onion with you to keep off diseases. You can't take a disease from any odor that the onion scent is strong enough to overcome so that you don't smell it. Indeed, whatever you can't smell won't harm you, onion or no onion. But if you think you smell a disease, even if you don't, you are liable to have that disease.

A good way to keep from having cramps is to wear an eelskin around your ankle.

If you want to go to sleep and can't, count up to twenty-three hundred.

If that doesn't work, just imagine a crow flying round and round up in the sky in large circles.

Sleep with a piece of steel under your pillow, and you will not have rheumatism. I have heard of one woman who always put her scissors under her pillow, when bedtime came, for this purpose.

"Do you ever have the nightmare? Well, sir, my father used to have the nightmare right along every night. He'd be all of a didder -- shakin' and shudderin' till my mother'd take hold of him and wake him up. That'd bring him right out of 'em."

"One time he went away from home, and it come night and they was sittin' around in the tavern bar-room, and he told one o' the men there that he really dreaded to go to bed. He told him how he always had the nightmare, and how, bein' away from home, he wouldn't have his wife to wake him up. He said he was afraid he might die in it.

"'Well,' says the man, 'I'll tell you a cure for that; and if it don't work when you try it to-night, I'll stand drinks for the crowd in the mornin'. If it does work, you c'n stand the drinks.'

"So the man says, 'Now, when you go to bed, you just smell your stockin's after you take 'em off. That's all you've got to do, and you won't have no nightmare to-night, I'll warrant you.'

"Father did it, and it was just as the man said. Now, if any of your friends have the nightmare, you want to tell 'em of that, and theyll thank ye for it when they've found out how sure it cures 'em."

If your right nostril bleeds, you can stop it by tying a cord tight around your left little finger. If it is your left nostril that bleeds, tie the cord around the right little finger.

"My brother used to be quite a hand to hav cramps. Finally some one told him that when he had 'em he must wet his finger, and make a cross right on the calf of his leg. He done it, and it cured him every time. He says he don't know of anything better'n that for cramps."

A good many people have an idea that a person enjoys better health, and lives longer, if he is in the habit of sleeping with his head to the north. The important point is not that the head is to the north, but that the electric pole is in that direction.

Some people prefer to sleep with the head to the east. It is in that direction that the earth turns, and they think it healthier to be projected through space head first.

Wear a tarred string around your neck to keep from taking contagious diseases.

If your eyes are weak, have your ears bored just as you would for earrings. That will help make your eyes strong.

You can cure another person's headache by rubbing the aching one's head. The headache will presently leave the sufferer, and you will have it yourself, but less severely. A rheumatic shoulder treated in the same way brings the same results.

****

Bill Nye (Edgar Wilson Nye) was one of the most famous and beloved comic writers of the last century. He was born in Maine in 1850, grew up on a Wisconsin farm, then moved west to Laramie, Wyoming, to work for the *Laramie Daily Sentinel* in 1876.

In 1877, he passed the bar and began the practice of law. But that life was not for him, a born newspaperman. He quit the law to edit a new newspaper in Laramie from 1881-1883.

He contracted spinal meningitis and was forced to move to a different climate, choosing Wisconsin, where he died in 1886.

THE OPIUM HABIT

I have always had a horror of opiates of all kinds. They are so seductive and so still in their operations. They steal through the blood like a wolf on the trail, and they seize upon the heart at last with their white fangs till it is still forever.

Up the Laramie there is a cluster of ranches at the base of the Medicine Bow, near the north end of Sheep Mountain, and in sight of the glittering, eternal frost of the snowy range. These ranches are the homes of the young men from Massachusetts, Pennsylvania and Ohio, and now there are several "younger sons" of Old England, with herds of horses, steers and sheep, worth millions of dollars. These young men are not of the kind of whom the metropolitan ass writes as saying "youbetcher-life," and calling everybody "pardner." They are many of them college graduates, who can brand a wild Maverick or furnish the easy gestures for a Strauss waltz.

They wear human clothes, talk in the United States language, and have a bank account. This spring they may be wearing chaparajos and swinging a quirt through the thin air, and in July they may be at Long Branch, or coloring a meerschaum pipe among the Alps.

Well, a young man whom we will call Curtis lived at one of these ranches years ago, and, though a quiet, mind-your-own-business fellow, who had absolutely no enemies among his companions, he had the misfortune to incur the wrath of a tramp sheep-herder, who waylaid Curtis one afternoon and shot him dead as he sat in his buggy. Curtis wasn't armed. He didn't dream of trouble till he drove home from town, and, as he passed through the gates of a corral, saw the hairy face of the herder, and at the same moment the flash of a Winchester rifle. That was all.

The rancher came into town and telegraphed to Curtis's father, and then a half dozen citizens went out to help capture the herder, who had fled to the sage brush of the foot-hills.

They didn't get back till toward daybreak, but they brought the herder with them. I saw him in the gray of the morning, lying in a coarse gray blanket, on the floor of the engine house. He was dead.

I asked, as a reporter, how he came to his death, and they told me--opium! I said, did I understand you to say "ropium?" They said no, it was opium. The murderer had taken poison when he found that escape was impossible.

I was present at the inquest, so that I could report the case. There was very little testimony, but all the evidence seemed to point to the fact that life was extinct, and a verdict of death by his own hand was rendered.

It was the first opium work I had ever seen, and it aroused my curiosity. Death by opium, it seems, leaves a dark purple ring around the neck. I did not know this before. People who die by opium also tie their hands together before they die. This is one of the eccentricities of opium poisoning that I have ever seen laid down in the books, I bequeath it to medical science. Whenever I run up against a new scientific discovery, I just hand it right over to the public without cost.

Ever since the above incident, I have been very apprehensive about people who seem to be likely to form the opium habit. It is one of the most deadly of narcotics, especially in a new country. High up in the pure mountain atmosphere, this man could not secure air enough to prolong life, and he expired. In a land where clear, crisp air and delightful scenery are abundant, he turned his back upon them both and passed away. Is it not sad to contemplate?

****

Will Rogers dabbled in stories about miracle cures, a popular topic in his day. Here he describes the curative waters from the town near the ranch where he was born. Thus, you can depend on the authenticity of the story!

As you know, Mr. Rogers was fond of tall tales. In fact, he may have been the one who invented another word for them...whoppers.

Here is his tale, slightly condensed, from the great collection of his stories, *Illiterate Digest*, (A.L. Burt Co., N.Y., 1923).

"IF YOU DON'T GET WELL AND THROW AWAY YOUR CRUTCHES I GET NOTHING OUT OF IT."

TAKING THE CURE BY THE SHORES OF
CAT CREEK

Now, in my more or less checkered career before the more or less checkered Public, I have been asked to publicly indorse everything from Chewing Gum, Face Beautifiers, Patent Cocktail Shakers, Ma Junk Sets, even Corsets, Cigarettes, and Chewing Tobacco, all of which I didn't use or know anything about. But I always refused.

You never heard me boosting for anything, for I never saw anything made that the fellow across the street didn't make something just as good.

But, at last, I have found something that I absolutely know no one else has something just as good as, for an all-seeing Nature put this where it is and it's the only one he had, and by a coincidence it is located in the Town near the ranch where I was born and raised.

So I hereby and hereon come out unequivocally (I think that's the way you spell it) in favor of a place that has the water that I *know* will cure you. You might ask, cure me of what? Why, cure you of anything--just name your disease and dive in.

You might wonder how we discovered this Blarney Stone of Waters. In the early days, us old timers there, always considered these Wells more as an Odor than as a Cure. But one day a man come in there who had been raised in Kansas and he had heard in a roundabout way of people bathing, although he had never taken one. So, by mistake, he got into this Radium Water.

He was a one armed man--he had lost an Arm in a rush to get into a Chautauqua Tent in Kansas to hear Bryan speak on Man Vs. Monkey. Well he tried this Bath and it didn't kill him and he noticed that he was beginning to sprout a new arm where he had lost the old one, so he kept on with the Baths and it's to him that we owe the discovery of this wonderful curative Water. Also he was the Pioneer of Bathers of Kansas, as now they tell me it's no uncommon thing to have a Tub in most of their larger towns.

Now, it has been discovered that you can carry a thing too far and overdo it, so we don't want you there too long. A man come there once entirely Legless and stayed a week too long and went away a Centipede.

I want to offer here my personal Testimonial of what it did to me. You see, after this Kansas Guy started it, why, us old Timers moved our bathing from the River into a Tub. Now, at that time, I was practically Tongue tied and couldn't speak out in private much less in Public. Well, after 12 baths, I was able to go to New York and make after dinner speeches. I stopped in Washington on the way and saw how our Government was run and that gave me something funny to speak about.

So, in thanking the Water, I also want to thank the Government for making the whole thing possible. Now, had I taken 24 baths I would have been a Politician, so you see I stopped just in time.

The only thing I get out of this is I have the "Thrown Away Crutch Privilege." If you don't get well and throw away your Invalid Chair or crutches I get nothing out of it, so that is why we give you a square deal. If you are not cured, I don't get your Crutches. There is no other resort in the World that works on that small a margin.

W. J. Bryan drank one drink of this Water and turned against Liquor. Senator La Follette drank two drinks of it and turned against everything. So remember Claremore, The Carlsbad of America, where the 'Frisco Railroad crosses the Iron Mountain Railroad, not often, but every few days.

****

Doctor jokes are not new. Some go back to the ancient Greeks. Here are four from a 1910 jokebook. It seems safe to conclude that the physician-as-target for jokes good, bad and indifferent, is by no means a recent phenomenon.

The Doctor

Smith, who had always been a "tough one," had just died. The physician is met coming from the house by Brown, who asks, "Doctor, how is Smith? Is he out of danger?" Physician: "No. He is dead, poor fellow; but he is far from being out of danger, I fear."

A young physician, proud of his three-days'-old diploma, was gleefully telling a physician of many years' experience of his luck in being appointed to the staff of one of the big Brooklyn hospitals.

"Just to think of it!" said the young man. "Here I am only a few days out of college, too. I expect to learn a whole lot in that hospital."

"Yes," said the old campaigner. "I know of no better place to confirm your diagnosis by an autopsy."

Doctor: "What? Troubled with sleeplessness? Eat something before going to bed."

Patient: "Why, doctor, you once told me never to eat anything before going to bed."

Doctor (with dignity): "Pooh, pooh! That was last January. Science has made enormous strides since then."

The millionaire had been very ill, but the doctor's smile was cheerful and encouraging.

"At last, my very dear sir," he said, grasping the patient's nerveless hand, "at last, I am happy to say, that you are completely out of danger."

"No risk of a relapse?"

"None whatever."

"Break it gently to my poor nephew," whispered the invalid faintly.

****

An epitaph for Peter Daniels (1688-1746) who jumped the gun a month or so:

> Beneath this stone, a lump of clay,
> Lies Uncle Peter Daniels,
> Who too early in the month of May -
> Took off his winter flannels.

****

Irving Cobb (1876-1944) was one of the all-time great American humorists. These selections are from his *A Laugh A Day Keeps the Doctor Away*. Garden City Publishers, 1923.

A country girl went to Charleston, South Carolina, to have some work done on her teeth. The operator was cleansing a cavity with a small blow-pipe. The patient flinched.

"Do you feel that air?" asked the dentist.

"That air whut?" said the young lady.

The eminent Dr. Blank, specialist in bone and muscular diseases, was a busy man. The routine in his offices was devised with a view to facilitating the handling of cases. He had a full staff of nurses, clerks and attendants.

On a certain morning a neatly dressed and diffident-appearing youth entered the outer room and told the nurse in charge that he wished to see Dr. Blank.

"Have you an appointment?" she asked.

"No, ma'am," he said.

"Then this must be your first visit?"

"Yes, ma'am."

"Very well, then. Go to that dressing-room down the hall, second door on the left, and remove all your clothing, including your shoes. Presently a bell will ring and you may then enter the adjoining room where Dr. Blank will be waiting to see you."

Blushingly, the young man started to say that he didn't think all this was necessary. With an authoritative gesture the nurse checked him.

"If you really desire to see Dr. Blank you must do exactly as I tell you," she stated. "This is the invariable rule for all who call upon him for the first time."

Still protesting, the stranger repaired to the disrobing chamber. Sure enough, within a few minutes a bell tinkled, and, wearing nothing at all except his embarrassment, the youth stepped timorously across a threshold into an inner room where the distinguished specialist sat at a desk.

"Well sir," snapped the expert with professional brusqueness, "what seems to be the matter with you?"

"There ain't nothin' the matter with me," said the newcomer.

"Well, then, what do you want? What did you come here for?"

"I came," said the youth, "to see if you didn't want to renew your subscription to the *Ladies Home Journal*."

Dr. Jones, a young physician with a growing practice, had been going night and day for the better part of a week. If it wasn't the stork busy in one part of the town it was the malaria microbe busy in another. He kept up his round of visits until exhausted nature demanded a respite.

He staggered into his house in the evening completely fagged out, and tumbled into bed, telling his wife that, excepting upon a matter of life and death, he was not to be called.

At two o'clock in the morning she came to his bedside, shook him, pinched him, slapped him in the face with a wet washrag and finally roused him to a state of semi-consciousness. Mrs. Smith, physically the biggest woman in town, had been seized with a heart attack at her home on the next street and he was wanted immediately.

He struggled to his feet, threw a few garments on over his night-clothes, caught up his emergency kit and in a sort of walking trance made his way to the Smith residence. A frightened member of the household led him to the sick-room. There the patient lay, a great mountain of flesh, her features congested and her breath coming in laborious panting. Dr. Jones took her pulse and her temperature and examined her eyes, her lips and her tongue. Then he perched himself in a half recumbent attitude upon the side of the bed, put his right ear against her left breast and said:

"Madam, will you kindly start counting very slowly? Now then, one-two-three and so on. Go on until I tell you to stop."

Obediently the sufferer began.

The next thing Dr. Jones knew was when a shaft of bright morning sunlight fell upon his face, and, drowsily, he heard a faint, weak female voice saying:

"Nine-thousand-seven-hundred and one, nine-thousand-seven-hundred and two----!"

252

A literal and simple-minded man, by birth a German, sent his wife to the hospital for an operation. The operation was performed in the forenoon. In the afternoon, when he quit work, the husband called to inquire how the patient had stood the ordeal. The nurse told him that she seemed to be improving.

Early the next morning he was on hand asking for the latest tidings from the sick-room, and again he was informed that his wife still appeared to be improving. Twice daily all through the week he received similar reports.

But one morning when he called he was met with the distressing news that she had passed away. In a daze the widower started down the street to find an undertaking establishment. On the way he met an acquaintance and the latter said:

"Well, how's your wife to-day?"

"She iss dead," answered the bereft one.

"Ach!" said his friend. "That's too bad. I thought she was getting along first rate. What did she die of?"

"Improvements."

ACKNOWLEDGEMENT

We are indebted to Kathy Gallagher (Circulation Desk) and Marion Lucasik (Reference Librarian) of Southern Illinois University Medical School and to Mary Ellen McElligott of Springfield, Illinois, our proof reader.

BIBLIOGRAPHY

An Anthology of Dental Humor. Dr. Gerald Epstein. 1966. Dental Executive Associates. Westport, CT.

All I Ever Wanted Was A Piece of Cornbread And A Cadillac. Bo Whaley. 1989. Rutledge Hill Press. Nashville, TN.

Cartoon Annual. A. Wyn, Inc., Publisher. New York. Reprinted with permission of King Features Syndicate.

Cartoons by Dave Carpenter, Emmetsburg, IA.

Cartoons by James Estes, Amarillo, TX.

Cartoons by Lo Linkers, Mission, B.C. Canada.

Cartoons by Masters Agency, Hollister, CA.

Cartoons by Eldon Pletcher, Slidell, LA.

Cover of book reprinted with permission of copyright © 1930, The Curtis Publishing Co. Indianapolis, IN.

Coffee Break, Charles Preston, Editor. 1955. Cartoon Features Syndicate. Boston, MA.

Cracklin' Bread and Asfidity: Folk Recipes and Remedies, Jack and Olivia Solomon. The University of Alabama Press, Tuscaloosa, AL.

Dentists Are Funny People, Jeanne Chelsey, Editor. 1972. Gallery Books. Santa Monica, CA.

Foley's Footnotes: A Treasury of Dentistry. Gardner P.H. Foley. 1873. Washington Square East Publishers. Wallingford, PA.

For Doctor's Only. Dr. Francis Leo Golden. Frederick Fell, Inc., Publishers.

Hot Springs And Hell. Vance Randolph. 1965. Folklore Assoc. Hatboro, PA.

The Humor Of The American Cowboy. Stan Hoig. 1970. The University of Nebraska Press, Lincoln, NE.

Illinois Medical Journal. Illinois State Medical Society. Chicago, IL.

It All Started With Hippocrates. Richard Armour. 1966. McGraw-Hill Publication.

Just For The Fun Of It. Carl Goerch. 1954. Edwards & Broughton Co. Raleigh, NC.

Kiss A Mule, Cure A Cold. Evelyn Jones Childers. 1988. Peachtree Publications, Ltd. Atlanta, GA.

Laughing Matters. The Humor Project, Inc. Saratoga Springs, NY.

Let's Go To Bedlam. Charles Preston, Editor. Shelley Publishing Co. New York.

Man The Beast. Virgil Franklin Partch. 1953. Little, Brown and Company. Boston, MA.

Medical Economics Magazine. Montvale, NJ.

The Medical Muse. Richard Armour. 1963. McGraw-Hill Book Co. New York.

More Over Sexteen. J. M. Elgart. 1963. Grayson Publishing Co.

Never Try To Teach A Pig To Sing. Alan Dundes and Carl R. Pagter. Wayne State University Press. Detroit, MI.

The New England Journal of Medicine. Waltham, MA.

Ode To The Circumcised Male. Edgar J. Schoen, M.D.

Over Sexteen. J. M. Elgart. 1958. Grayson Publishing Co.

The Record. Yale University. New Haven, CT.

Saturday Evening Post. Indianapolis, IN.

Surviving The Cure. Janet Henry. Cope, Inc. Cleveland, OH.

That's Incurable. George Thomas, M.D. and Lee Schreiner, M.D. 1984. Viking Penguin, NY.

There Ought To Be A Law. Don Herold. 1926. E. P. Dutton & Co., A division of Penguin Books USA, Inc.

Theta Kappa Psi. Chicago, IL.

The Unofficial Nurse's Handbook. Richard Mintzer and Nina Schroeder. 1986. Ultra Communications, Inc., a Division of Penguin Books, USA, Inc.

We Always Lie To Strangers. Vance Randolph. 1951. Columbia University Press. New York.

What The Old Timer Said And Then Some. Allen Foley. 1983. Stephen Greene Press, an imprint of Penguin Books USA, Inc.

What The Queen Said. Stoddard King. Doubleday. New York.

Whinorrhea: New Understanding Of An Old Problem. Elizabeth Schultz, R.N., B.S.N. and Bob Quick - Cartoon.